All Things Beautiful
INSIDE & OUT

YOUR BEAUTY GUIDE TO WHOLENESS

LaDONNA D. ROBERTS

Paperback ISBN: 978-1-63616-076-4
Ebook ISBN: 978-1-63616-077-1

Published By Opportune Independent Publishing Co.
www. opportunepublishing.com
Best-Selling Author Coach: Nikkie Pryce

Printed in the United States of America
For permission requests, email the author with the subject line as "Attention: Permissions Coordinator" to the email address below:

ladonna@robertsmgmt.co

Book Dedication

To my Lord and Savior, Jesus Christ. You are in a category all by Yourself! I am GRATEFUL for the inspiration You gave me to encourage and empower your daughters!

To Both of my parents
Charles A. Brown and Donna J. Monroe, you two inspired a great deal of content contained in this book. I know both of you are cheering me on from heaven!

Dear Uncle Arthur (Buzzy)
Uncle, you loved and cared for me from the very start. You are loved more than you'll ever know!

Amplified Bible

"[11] He has made everything beautiful and appropriate in its time. He has also planted eternity [a sense of divine purpose] in the human heart [a mysterious longing which nothing under the sun can satisfy, except God]—yet man cannot find out (comprehend, grasp) what God has done (His overall plan) from the beginning to the end."

Ecclesiastes 3:11

Table of Contents

Acknowledgement   **9**
Introduction   **11**
Chapter 1: Matters Of The Heart   **17**
Harboring pain that holds you back
My pain, my triumph
Why forgiveness is essential
Chapter 2: Faith   **53**
Finding your Identity
Know who you are in Christ
Who does God say that you are?
Chapter 3: Self-Care   **65**
Balance
Mental Health
Celebrating your wins
Chapter 4: Outward Beauty   **77**
Eyelash Enhancements
Eyebrows Enhancements
Make-Up
Chapter 5: Lifestyle   **95**
Hosting for Small Gathering
Chapter 6: Marriage Preparation   **115**
Proper Christian Dating
Characteristics of a Godly Man
Boundaries
About The Author   **129**

All Things Beautiful

Acknowledgments

My wonderful, supportive, AMAZING husband, Ronald L. Roberts, Sr. that allows me to do what God has called me to do. My three sons, Johnathan, Ronald Jr, and Geo, my two daughters, Jolie and Christian, who are my absolute heartbeats who have collectively blessed me with 4 "GrandGirls" as of now, Taylor, Charlie, Zoe, and Naima that are my PURE joy! Also to my goddaughter, Trinity, godsons, Tabari, Jason, Darrell, and Isaiah. All of my sisters, sister/cousin, sisters-in-love, nieces, cousins, my sister from another mother, my bestie Lafayetta, I am so Grateful to God that He chose me to be the answer to your prayer for a friend that is no different than a sister. To all my sister-friends (You KNOW who you are), who's relation I DON'T take lightly nor for granted, I Love You. To my confidants and warrior princesses, and every woman that's reading this right now, to my "No Quit" Coach, Rhonda Culton who inspired this book. But it became clear to me, that I needed some hand holding. If it had not been for my "90-Day Best-Selling Author Coach Nikkie Pryce, you probably wouldn't be holding this book in your hands yet. Coach Nikkie was very methodical in her approach to the success of getting my book written, and published, I cannot Thank you enough.

To Prophetess Kathleen Cade I want to THANK YOU for every prayer, declaration, and prophetic word and/

or instruction given, but more importantly your love. My amazing bonus mom, Minnie Davis, and the best mother-in-love anyone can ever hope to have,
Hazel M. Roberts.

Last but certainly not least, my spiritual parents,
Dr. Lovy and Prophetess Maggy Elias and Dr. Prophetess, Taryn N. Tarver,
Truly, my life has never been the same.

I Love You ALL for supporting and loving me the way you do.
THANK YOU, Immensely!

Introduction

Greetings! My name is LaDonna, and I'll be your Beauty Mentor throughout this guide, serving you as you intentionally take this journey through an investigative discovery of your authentic self.

When I say, "I believe everything you touch with intention can be made beautiful." I believe it starts with being made whole. Beauty is an inside job first. External beauty with internal brokenness and unforgiveness can cause you to be bound and unavailable, both emotionally and spiritually. The problem is that many women of faith have internal bleeding that no one knows about because we have mastered masquerading, stuffing, and numbing ourselves. I invite you to permit yourself to discover your real authentic self and come forth. You are so much more than just another "pretty face."

In this Beauty Guide, I will take you through "All Things Beautiful Inside & Out."

But first, let me share how this all started. As far back as I can remember, I have always been a heart person. I had an internal default towards wanting things around me to be better, look better, be more loving, kinder, more peaceful, balanced, and be made beautiful.

My mother was a beautiful woman. When she was the age that most of you are right now, she would always have every strand of hair in place, and on days she couldn't pull it together, she wore turbans that complemented whatever stylish outfit she'd chosen for the day. Even when she was around the house, she would wear beautiful caftans (a long loose dress) ever before, just putting on a robe. Her makeup regime was very light. Less was more for her but was always the cherry on top. I remember that being one of the highlights of my day was to sit and watch her in awe. I was very susceptible to the environment around me; I never liked voice elevation (arguing), tension, unfair treatment, items in disarray, messiness, sadness, or heartbreak. So, even as a young girl, "All Things Beautiful Inside & Out" was what I sought. Whether it was my physical surroundings, making people feel better emotionally, or problem-solving, I was always the happiest when I made a difference.

As I got older, I was acutely aware that forgiveness was NOT being served up on a plater; it wasn't extended, solicited, or received. Quite frankly, it seemed as though most people were angry at someone and not genuinely happy. Way before "Rodney King," I just wanted everybody to get along, not just to go along to get along…but indeed be free and unencumbered, not carrying the heaviness that unforgiveness brings. With that, it's no surprise that I gravitated unknowingly to professions that supported my efforts to make a difference in all the areas close to my heart. I started in Banking and Finance, balancing essential internal controls and reconciling to prevent fraud and identify errors to be quickly corrected. Then, I went into auditing to show accurate and fair views of the company's financial position. Do you see the parallels? Balance, reconciliation, fairness. Even as I shifted into the beauty industry, I loved external beauty as well. I became an esthetician, make-up artist, certified Christian mentor, and accredited event designer. By the time this book is published and released, I will add licensed minister and, soon after, certified life coach. All of those experiences have brought me to where I am today, cultivating and inspiring beauty inside and out.

Now, right through here, I want to pull up a virtual chair as if we are in a room together with a delicious cup of coffee/ tea and tissues with all transparency and vulnerability. Our time together here is for the sole purpose of sharing my heart and telling you what I had to walk through. People assume you've never gone through anything when you don't look like what you've been through. Well, that's not my testimony. I never wanted anyone to think that heaven unzipped, and I dropped out and started walking.

Growing up, I had two sisters and one brother that I was raised with. The four of us had different fathers. At this time in my life, I hadn't met my father yet; that happened when I was 13 years of age. As a young child, my mother was married to my eldest sister's father. What I remember about him the most was that he was physically abusive to my mother.

Whenever he was intoxicated, he would become aggressive, and that's when he would assault her, then he would leave. I would run to her aid to wipe away her tears until he came back, then I would run back to my room and pray. One of the prayers was that he would never come back, and the second prayer was that I wouldn't marry the wrong person. I was always afraid that things might get really bad for her/us. One day, he called me into their room, where he would always watch those cartoons that had very few Words like Road Runner and Pink Panther; that's when he was the happiest. He said, "come watch cartoons with me."

I'm sure it was welcomed since I hadn't known the love or touch of a father, so I did. He said, "let's snuggle." I remember him drawing me to him and me laying my head on his chest. He started rubbing my back and pulling me even closer... then his hand began to roam, and then placed my hand on him, asking me to rub his private parts while telling me how good it made him feel. He then tried to enter me and couldn't because I said it hurt, so he didn't force it. At that moment, I didn't want to aggravate him by "complaining" because he said, "it made him feel so good." I didn't know what his triggers were. I thought since he "felt so good," maybe he wouldn't hurt my mother again, so I endured it all. He told me I shouldn't say anything because he didn't want to upset my Mom. I wasn't sure what emotions I felt outside of fear and trauma because I was only around 7 or 8 years of age.

Shortly after that, he moved out unannounced. My mother was at work, and he told us all to play outside in the front. Little did we know, he had a moving truck in the alley behind us and later found out that he brought his "girlfriend," and they cleaned the house out.

I don't even remember what my mother's reaction was when she came home! I remember being very happy that he couldn't hurt my mom or touch me anymore.

He is currently still alive in his 80s or 90's, and I have not seen him in my adult years. When I began to write this book, I knew I wanted to help young women be free from the pain, violations, and unforgiveness in their past and present. I shared my trauma with my sister a while back, but I wanted her to know that I felt like other young women needed to hear about my story. I was very concerned about how she would view him since she saw him frequently. My sister and I earnestly prayed that he would ask God for forgiveness and receive Jesus Christ as Lord and Savior before he leaves this earth.

Many of you may have a similar story, being violated in some way, whether physically, emotionally, or even spiritually. For many years into my adult years, that's something I put out of my head, not fully aware of its effect on me. I then decided to intentionally sit with it to locate how I really felt about it. You see, I did the very thing I'm encouraging you to do…I decided to CHOSE to extend forgiveness to someone who would probably never say he was sorry or ever solicit it. It's my freedom and MY CHOICE.

I promise you that if you commit to this process and allow me to walk with you through this, take God at His Word; you can be made whole. The BIG question you may have is…How do you forgive?

The short answer is: You, in essence, decide and **CHOOSE** to forgive; it means to lay it aside; to let it alone; to cease to feel resentment; to clear the record, and not hold persons responsible. It doesn't mean that you entirely forget about the hurt, but you remember it without pain.

This book is for those that are ready to embrace the fullness of who God says you are and receive your inheritance so that you will be made whole, Inside and Out, as God intended.

This book is NOT for those who are not quite ready to allow God's Word to transform them so that they are free to carry out their purposes unshackled.

Don't delay by allowing fear of the unknown to grip you, fear of feeling the emotions and pain of the past as you journey along to wholeness.

Although I share some great tips and valuable resources with you throughout the book for external beauty, please personalize the process by being interactive at the end of each chapter and capturing what you discovered about yourself. There may be areas or topics that will be touched with the intention that may be more challenging than others to journey through to wholeness, but your beauty coach is here with you.

I am so excited to take this journey along with you! At the back of the book, you'll find all the ways to connect with me. Please share your experience with me. I would love to hear about how God met you where you were on your journey to wholeness and internal beauty, even if you feel you may need additional support. Also, share if you picked up some external beauty tips to incorporate as well!

May God's AMAZING Grace overtake you!

Chapter 1
Matters Of The Heart

Harboring Pain That Holds You Back

Let me give you a real-life scenario; we'll call her "Sherri." Sherri grew up in a single-parent home. Her father abandoned her and her mom when she was only five years old. Sherri's mom tried her best to nurture her with confidence and love her the best way she knew how. A single mom also raised Sherri's mom. So the hurt and bitterness towards men often surfaced as Sherri got older.

Elementary school was no walk in the park, as she had to work twice as hard as her friends, who benefited from living with both their parents. Despite all the challenges, she always remembered her grandmother's prayers and declarations over her growing up. Sherri held on to her faith in God, and this helped her through many dark days.

At the age of 31, Sherri had experienced more hardship and heartbreak than many people experience in a lifetime. She faced abuse, depression, abandonment, betrayal, and low self-esteem. When it seemed as though her life couldn't get any worse, Sherri met and fell in love with the man of her dreams- or so she thought. Getting married at the age of 29 was a dream come true for Sherri; this was what she envisioned for her life from 12 years old. Marrying a pastor's son and someone active in ministry only added to her bliss and happiness.

'Was this the turning point in my life that I was waiting for?' Sherri thought.

She was very happy and thankful to God that her life did not mirror her mother and grandmother before. Now she had a man who loved God and loved her. She was ecstatic.

To her dismay, her long-awaited happiness only lasted for two short years. Her deep-seated anger, bitterness, and resentment for her father and all who had hurt her frequently surfaced in her marriage. This led her husband to ask for a trial separation as he became overwhelmed with receiving the brunt of her anger.

Like many hurting women today, Sherri had many emotional scars that left her vulnerable and open to unforgiveness, bitterness and resentment. Until she intentionally and deliberately dealt with and overcame those issues, she would forever live beneath her God-ordained purpose.

Sherri's heart was scarred by the many persons that hurt her in the past. Sherri will never be fully free until she let go and allows God to completely heal her heart. She will not be able to adequately love and support her husband as his 'help-meet'. She will not be able to mother her children like a 'Proverbs 31' woman. She will not be able to serve others unreservedly in the way God has purposed for her life.

A lot of us are in the same position as Sherri. We are holding on to past hurt, which has crippled us from moving forward in our lives and ministries. Many like Sherri have faced heartbreak, heartaches, abuse, abandonment, depression, bitterness, and resentment. If we are honest with ourselves, we will also admit that it does feel good sometimes to hold on to the grudges, wishing that one day we will get our revenge on those that have wronged us.

As the saying goes, 'revenge is best served cold.' However, no matter how good it feels to want to get back at those that have caused us pain, this is not God's way.

Holding on to unforgiveness is detrimental to our emotional stability and our spiritual growth and maturity. The condition of one's heart is just as important in the spirit as it is in the natural. The Bible has so much to say about the heart. That is why it is so crucial for us to guard it against unforgiveness and bitterness. Proverbs 4:23 tells us to 'Keep our heart with all diligence; for out of it are the issues of life.'

It is so easy for us to hold on to past hurt. Luke 17:1 tells us that offenses will come. That simply means there is not one human being on the face of this earth that will not feel offended by others and struggle with unforgiveness. There comes a time in all of our lives that we contend with dealing with unforgiveness. One of the important things that we all have to learn in our life is how to forgive.

In essence, you choose to forgive; it means to lay it aside; to let it alone; to cease to feel resentment; to clear the record, and not to hold persons responsible. It doesn't mean that you fully forget about the hurt, but you remember it without pain.

Because of the many times Sherri was hurt in her life, she was so easily offended- she struggled with unforgiveness. She thought that everyone was out to get her and that no one could be trusted. It was so easy for her to get irritated and resentful. Many of us are not much different from Sherri. Someone could just be looking at you, and you get offended, and it is the seed of offense that breeds unforgiveness.

1 Corinthians 13: 5 tells us that love "Doth not behave itself unseemly, seeketh not her own, is not easily provoked, thinketh no evil" If we are truly working in love, it doesn't matter what your background is, you will not be easily angered.

If we don't forgive, it affects our relationship with God. Unforgiveness is a product of judging things from the lens of your own perception of yourself. When you judge things from a faulty perception, things will be interpreted from the lens of your own limitation. As children of God, we must refuse to be offended. We must make up our mind that the blessings we seek to receive from the relationships God brings in our lives are greater than any offense or unforgiveness. Like Sherri, many people have lost precious relationships because of unforgiveness, bitterness, and offense. You mustn't allow what other people do to you to impact your relationship with God. Harboring unforgiveness makes you small. It's typical for us to harbor feelings of bitterness, resentment, anger, and unforgiveness when we have been hurt. Still, no matter the situation or who was at fault, we always seem to concoct in our minds the 'what-if's and should haves'.' What if I had done this' or 'I should have said that. It's human to want to analyze and re-evaluate the past, but one major component to emotional healing is facing reality, forgiving yourself and the other party, and moving on.

The loss of any relationship can be one of the most stressful and emotional experiences that we face in our lives, but regardless of the reason for that separation - work, marriage, friendship - it tends to turn your whole world into a tailspin and trigger all types of unpleasant emotional feelings.

When we are faced with the reality that our life is not what we expected it to be and things just don't seem to make sense, we grapple with undeniable feelings of emotional and psychological turmoil. We now have to pick up the shattered pieces of our lives and move forward, but how do we do this?

We experience deep disappointment, stress, and grief, which can affect our daily lives at work, at home, among our friends, or at church. It so often also affects our self-perception. Like Sherri, some feel as though what happened to them is their fault and are now battling low self-esteem.

You may be wondering if you will ever be able to recover from this hurt. You are wondering if your life will ever be normal. Psalm 23:3 reassures us that God restores our soul, heals our heart and renews our spirit despite what we went through and how we are feeling. He will restore your joy, your peace, and your contentment. If we are to walk in wholeness and forgive others, it is imperative for us to forgive ourselves and to know that even though we are going through this situation now, it is not the end for us. God has better plans ahead, and He promises to make all things beautiful in His time.

What is forgiveness? Forgiveness is giving. It is giving pardon and mercy. It is when you are ready to let go even before the offense happens. It is a dimension of giving. If you are not a forgiver, you are not a giver.

Forgiving yourself can be difficult, and it takes time. However, it's important to keep reminding yourself that you can and will get through this difficult season of your life by the grace of God. God, through the Holy Spirit, will give you the strength to move on with a renewed sense of hope and optimism.

Forgiving yourself means that you have to let go of the negative feelings you have about yourself and replace them with positive affirmations. The bible says you are 'fearfully and wonderfully made'; 'you are the apple of God's eye'. So regardless of what happened in your past, leave it behind; give your struggles, fears, and heartaches to the Lord and embrace God's best for your life.

Now that you've forgiven yourself, you must forgive those who have caused you harm. It is equally important for you to extend forgiveness as you desire to be forgiven. God commands us to forgive others as He has forgiven us. It may be very difficult to forgive someone that has caused you much hurt, aggravation, and pain, but with the help of the Holy Spirit, you can forgive them. This will not come naturally and will take much effort on your part, but it is possible. Jesus is our ultimate example of forgiveness. What He endured for us on Calvary's cross shows us that we, too, can extend forgiveness no matter how challenging it may seem.

We have all been in situations where we have done wrong and desire forgiveness from someone- a friend, a sibling, a neighbor, a co-worker, or even a stranger. Then there are times when someone requires us to forgive them. We then have to look deeply within ourselves to offer it freely. It is not easy, but it is a powerful thing to extend to someone who might not even deserve it. The Bible gives us guidance as to how to forgive, and if we are to walk in obedience to what God commands, we must look beyond our hurt and forgive. When we forgive, we release the blessings of God upon our lives and we are free from all emotional baggage.

The hard truth is if we desire to walk in God's blessings and favor, we must obey His Word; we must forgive. The Lord makes it crystal clear in His Word that forgiveness is a command and not a mere suggestion. However, you don't have to do it on your own. Ask the Lord to help you, and He will heal every hurt and give you the strength you need to forgive. Even when it seems like you don't have the ability to forgive, you can rely on the Lord. *Philippians 4:13 assures us that 'we can do all things through Christ who strengthens us.'*

Forgiving those that wronged you will make you free from all feelings and thoughts of hatred, resentment, and bitterness. Forgiveness is not only done for the sake of the one you are forgiving, but it is also for your own sake so that you can be relieved of that burden and move on to enjoy what God has in store for you in the next season of your life.
Give yourself time to heal.

True healing comes through the Holy Spirit, and He will heal your heart and mend the broken pieces of your life. However, it is important to submit yourself to the process of healing and allow the Lord to restore you as He desires to do. Moving past your feelings of hurt and heartache to a place of healing is the ultimate end goal. So as you travel down the road to emotional recovery, it is important not to dwell on the negative feelings or to over-analyze the situation.

Dwelling on hurtful feelings like blame, anger, and resentment will rob you of valuable time and energy and will prevent you from experiencing God's supernatural healing and restoration.

Taking the time to re-discover yourself is vital to the healing process. The good news is, 'the Lord will perfect that which concerns you,' and He is with you in the process.

Remember that what you face now will not last forever, and His grace is sufficient for you, and His strength is made perfect in your weakness. The Bible admonishes in *Proverbs 3 verses 5-6 to 'trust in the Lord with all your heart and not to lean on your own understanding, but in all your ways acknowledge Him and He will direct your path'.*

God's timing is not our timing, but His timing is perfect, so I implore you to commit your situation to Him and watch Him move mightily in your life.

It is the Lord's will that we live higher than offense, higher than unforgiveness. We must reject unforgiveness. Make up your mind to practice forgiveness. *Mark 11:25 declares 'And when ye stand praying, forgive if ye have ought against any: that your Father also which is in heaven may forgive you your trespasses.'*

No relationship, including our relationship with God, can thrive without forgiveness. God continually forgives us of our sins, so we are to forgive those who have offended or done us wrong. It is amazing how we hold people for ransom in our hearts that have hurt us. It's like a small child that begs you for something, then you give it to him and say give me, and they refuse. We can never live in this life without forgiveness.

We don't just forgive to make peace. Forgiving to make peace is one of the benefits of forgiveness, but the primary purpose is to release yourself so you can move forward. A lack of forgiveness will affect your health, your relationships, and your walk with God.

When we have unforgiveness in our hearts, we cannot move forward. We release those that have wronged us so that we can move on to what the Lord has in store for us. Our responsibility is to have a disposition of forgiveness. People will offend you every day, people will do wrong things every day, but we must forgive. God gives us the grace to forgive.

You may say like Sherri, 'I will never forgive my father that abandoned me.' 'I will never forgive that spouse that deserted me!' 'I will never forgive my co-worker that betrayed me! 'I will never forgive that person who raped me! It is not easy, but the Lord wants you to forgive so that you can move forward. Release everyone who has offended you. Practice forgiveness. Luke 6:37

Entreats us, 'Judge not, and ye shall not be judged: condemn not, and ye shall not be condemned: forgive, and ye shall be forgiven:'

Colossians 3:13 states, 'Forbearing one another, and forgiving one another, if any man has a quarrel against any: even as Christ forgave you, so also do ye'. In partnership with forgiveness, we must also be tolerant. The reality is not everyone will be like us, and that is a good thing. We must see people as how God sees them. As God has looked beyond our faults, so we must also extend that same grace to others.

When we see others as Christ sees them, we will be aware that, in the same way we desire forgiveness, we also need to forgive others. All men are humans. We are frail and imperfect. We are debtors alone to the grace of God. We must desire to maintain a posture where we are not surprised at the behavior of people. Matthew 6:12 makes it clear that we get what we give. 'And forgive us our debts, as we forgive our debtors.'

The best of man is still a man. We are mere men helped by God. As we live this life, we must maintain an allowance for the humanity of men.

In Matthew 18:21-22, Peter said to Jesus, 'Lord, how often shall my brother sin against me, and I forgive him? till seven times? Jesus saith unto him, I say not unto thee, Until seven times: but, Until seventy times seven.'

We must sustain compassion in dealing with people. Men are human. Men are frail. Men are limited. That is true for men of God. That is true for business people. That is true for your boss in the office. That is true for your neighbor. That is true for your spouse, and that is true for you. Every time we do not give allowance for the humanity of men, we are sowing seeds, and the harvest will catch up with us. Forgiveness helps us break free from self-pity and experience God's peace. It puts you in a victorious position and removes you from a victim's position. God desires to heal your heart today. Whatever is overwhelming you, cast it at His feet and watch Him turn your life around.

My Prayer for You

Father, I worship, honor and exalt your Holy and matchless name. Lord, I thank you for your love and kindness toward me, and I ask that you purge my heart and make me more like you. I pray today for an outpouring of your Love, Healing, and Forgiveness.

Lord, you are love, and 1 Corinthians 13:1 tells us that if we don't have love, we are like sounding brass or a tinkling cymbal. So teach me how to love Lord.

Show me your ways, so I will live a life that mirrors your character and nature.

Father, in a world where people are indifferent toward each other, with political, racial and church division, may I exemplify true love and forgiveness as your child.

Lord, I know that love comes from you, and as *1 John 4:20 states, 'how can we say we love You who we can't see, yet hate our brother who we can see?'* Teach me, Lord, to put on Charity and walk as in the light and not in darkness.

I pray for those that feel unloved, despised, and rejected. May your All-encompassing love overshadow us right now in Jesus' name. May we experience your unconditional love as never before.

I pray for the hurting ones, the abused ones and the misused ones. We give you our hurt and pray that you take our pain and turn it into a praise report. You give beauty for ashes, so I give you all the ash-like situations in my life. I thank you that my hope is in you and not in another. Your Word says that if only we have hope in Christ in this life, then we are of all men most miserable. So I thank you that my hope is not in this world or of this world but is in YOU; my hope IS YOU.

I pray for hurting mothers, fathers, husbands, wives, sons, and daughters. When many are searching for answers in these uncertain times we are facing, I pray, Father, that you touch those depressed and discouraged. May the God of hope fill them with all joy, grace, and peace in Jesus' name.
Lord, it is because of your unmerited grace and love that we can experience what it is to truly be forgiven. I am grateful, Lord, that You have not dealt with us after our sins nor rewarded us according to our iniquities, but instead, you sent your son Jesus Christ to die for our sins.

Your Word tells us to forgive others as we have been forgiven, so Lord, give me the heart to forgive those that have wronged me. I release every person that has done me wrong. I reject every seed of rage and hatred in Jesus' name. I pray for those that are living with hearts filled with bitterness, resentment, and unforgiveness. May you heal them from every residue of hurt and disappointment that they too will be free to forgive others.

My desire, Lord, is to be like you and live my life to please you in every way. May I be the light that shines in this dark world, spreading love, joy, and forgiveness to everyone I come in contact with. Father, I give you my heart and life today, and I thank you for hearing me as I pray in Jesus' name. Amen.

My Pain, My Triumph
Healed Twice

It was in October 2010, and I had been increasingly feeling very tired, requiring more rest than usual. My sister and I owned a business in the Health and Beauty Industry in Los Angeles County. There was also another Wholistic Practitioner in the building that offered health screenings for Breast Cancer Awareness month. She continued to remind us to get SCREENING, so I complied on the last day, October 31st.

The report came back reading "MALIGNANT TERRAIN." I had just been diagnosed with Breast Cancer! IMMEDIATELY, I heard cancer in one ear and "Renegade Mutated Cell that Lacks Nutrition" in the other. I decided at that moment that I was going to break through and not break down. I never felt worried, anxious, or scared. My default was to hold on to God's unchanging hand like NEVER before! Now was when I had to activate my FAITH, believe God would do it FOR ME, and take Him at His Word! I KNEW that WITHOUT FAITH, IT IS IMPOSSIBLE to please Him! That would prove to be the day that my faith would be tested like NEVER before.

I immediately began to seek the Lord, asking what gave this infirmity entry or access, was it my diet, environmental, unforgiveness, bitterness, or EMOTIONAL DISTRESS. Bingo, emotional distress it was. The next question was, "Lord, What course do I take?". The Lord immediately gave ME a strategy for nourishing my body through prayer, holistic modalities, and nutrition. Then I had to begin to attack and dig up the ROOT that opened the door. I DID NOT broadcast it; I told a handful of people who would not pity me but would stand in POWER! I knew I had to fight from a place of VICTORY and NOT A VICTIM.

The year before, I received one of the most painful, devastating, and hurtful emails I HAD EVER received in my life, and it came from my mother. I was falsely accused of having a wrong motive in assisting her to relocate out of state. I was heartbroken and crushed. I tried to suck it up, but I was bleeding on the inside. That opened the door! Years prior, I was introduced to a "how-to formula," a kind of Biblical algebraic equation that produces that power for mountain-moving faith you can tap into for a manifested thing.

Mark 11:22-26 Amplified Bible:
22 Jesus replied, "Have Faith in God [constantly]. 23 I assure you and most solemnly say to you, whoever says to this mountain, 'Be lifted up and thrown into the sea!' and [a] does not doubt in his heart [in God's unlimited power], but believes that what he says is going to take place, it will be done for him [in accordance with God's will]. 24 For this reason I am telling you, whatever things you ask for in prayer [in accordance with God's will], believe [with confident trust] that you have received them, and they will be given to you. 25 Whenever you [b]stand praying, if you have anything against anyone, forgive him [drop the issue, let it go], so that your Father who is in Heaven will also forgive you your transgressions and wrongdoings [against Him and others]. 26 [c][But if you do not forgive, neither will your Father in Heaven forgive your transgressions."]

This Scripture written out as an algebraic equation would look like this:

$$PF \cdot S \,(-D + B)\, FG = THINGS \, ©$$

Pray in *faith* times *say* minus *doubt* plus *belief* times *forgiveness* equals *THINGS*.

Unforgiveness is a negative and will cancel out the whole equation.

In Mark 11:22, we're instructed to have Faith in God. $= F$

Verse 23 instructs us to say unto this mountain, (speak to the need). $= S$

Verse 23 also requires that one must have no doubt in his heart that what he says will come to pass and believe what he says. $= -D + B$

Verse 24 clarifies that our saying/speaking must be stated in faith unto God in prayer. $= P$

Verse 25 when you pray, forgive that God may forgive you. $= Fg$

Verse 26 says, if you do not forgive, your Father in Heaven will NOT forgive YOU.

Coach Al & Mrs. Hollingsworth., I can't thank you enough! The biblically based success training principles of B.O.S.S. The Movement and Vertical Leap have been embraced throughout the United States and the World. Al and Hattie Hollingsworth are the founders of the internationally acclaimed, Christ-centered youth success training curriculum and its adult success training component known as the Vertical Leap Seminar. This teaching, "From Faith to Things," and the mathematical equation, are copywritten material given to Coach Hollingsworth by God and taught in many countries. This teaching that I learned years prior was the one that proved to be my blueprint to wholeness.

Before we go to the main point, let's discover the meaning of faith.

Faith is a person's belief in the only true God without actually ever seeing Him in person. The dictionary defines faith as "belief, devotion, or belief in someone or something, especially for something that is not accompanied by logical evidence." Others define faith as "belief in and devotion to God." The Bible has a lot to say about faith and says how important it is to stand in it. In fact, it is so important that without faith, we can't please Him. (*Hebrews 11: 6*).

Faith could also be defined as a way of believing. Faith is a gift of God, worked out in the heart by the Holy Spirit, who quickens and guides all of our abilities towards one goal.

Faith is "*the foundation of things hoped for, and the evidence of things not seen*" (Hebrews 11: 1); Faith is the work of the soul by which we are confident of the existence and truth of something that is not in front of us, or invisible to all human senses. It is a practice of faith - a voluntary exercise - that enables us to grow in believing the great truths that God is pleased to reveal to us. Paul states, *"our life is by belief, not by sight."* (II Corinthians 5: 7).

Jesus Himself spoke (John 20:29), *"Blessed are those who do not see, yet believe."* Thus, while believing what we see and understand is beneficial, believing in what is invisible and only vaguely understood brings greater benefits. There are things in the world that we believe in without having to understand them fully; we believe because we get the evidence from other people, even if not from our own eye. Using faith will increase our spirituality, enabling us to understand things that would not be understood without this kind of practice. Paul said to educate Greeks who were skeptical of the Bible "foolishness." Pride in intelligence is one of the greatest hindrances to spiritual growth.

Advantages of Christian faith

"Faith is the substance of things hoped for, the evidence of things not seen" (Hebrews 11: 1).

Through faith, we obtain forgiveness of sins, justification, salvation, sanctification, adoption, and approach to God, the gift of the Holy Spirit, light and spiritual life, development, maintenance, eternal life, and rest in Heaven (Acts 10:43). Faith is essential for a beneficial understanding of the Gospel; this will make the Gospel more influential on believers; that faith is necessary for Christian warfare, and without faith, it is impossible to please the heart of God (Hebrews 4: 2; I Thessalonians 2:13).

Faith instills hope, peace, confidence, courage in preaching the Gospel and testifying and, as Christ is valuable to those who believe and abide in his heart, they live, stand, walk, get a "good testimony, *working with love, conquering the world, rejecting Satan*" (Romans 5: 2; Acts 16:34). Therefore, we must be earnest, steadfast, and faithful; hold fast to our faith with a good conscience and not only pray for improvement but with firm conviction (I Timothy 1: 5; II Corinthians 8: 7). Then we will be known by our fruits because without fruit, our faith is dead (James 2: 17, James 20-26), and because all difficulties are overcome by faith, so also all things must be done with it, without fear, for we are completely protected by our shields and armor (Matthew 17:20, 21:21; Romans 14:22).

<u>Our Main Focus is on the Book of Mark 5: 24-34</u>

The Bible tells us about a woman who had been bleeding for 12 years. She had been to many doctors and spent all her money on treatment, but instead of getting better, she was getting worse. Her situation was desperate. Due to her condition, she was considered an impure woman. This means that she had to stay isolated, alone, away from everyone: her family, friends, and neighbors. Everyone! For 12 years.

Can you imagine the pain she was experiencing on every

level? She had this physical condition she was suffering through. In addition, she had to bear the weight of the social stigma of being unclean. Her financial well-being was lost trying to find an answer to her infirmity. To make it all worse, she lost the emotional connectedness and love of her family and friends. Her condition altered her life in every way.

One day she heard about Jesus. She found out that He was near her home. Full of Faith and courage, she decided to take a risk and leave her home. Many people were surrounding Jesus, who was pushing on all sides, but she continued to advance. As she approached Jesus, she reached out her hand to touch his robe. She thought:

"If I can even touch his clothes, I'll be healthy." Instantly her bleeding stopped, and she realized that her body was free of that affliction.
(*Mark 5: 28-29*).

Jesus also realized that something supernatural had happened: He felt power come out of his body. He stopped, and looking around, asked who had touched Him. The disciples looked at Him and said they were all touching Him: they were in the middle of a crowd! But Jesus knew that the woman's touch had been different, one full of faith and hope.

Seeing that Jesus had realized this, the woman was filled with fear, knelt before Him, and confessed that it was her. Jesus replied:

"Daughter, your faith has healed you! Jesus said to her. Go in peace and be healed of all your affliction." (Mark 5:34).
The power of God was manifested amid that crowd! The

woman was healed of the ailment that had troubled her for 12 years.

"Never give up!" That is the character that appears in this woman. Imagine she has been suffering from bleeding for twelve years! I don't know how many healers she had visited to cure her but to no avail. She spent money on treatments and endured embarrassment as she passed through, yet she refused to give up.

This woman's story is the journey of faith confined in various conditions that weaken her. These situations require a faith that grows even in hopeless situations of illness, financial crises, and an uncertain future. It is a faith that grows amidst human limitations. It is a faith that moved mountains.

Believing in the power of the Lord Jesus and not giving up easily is also something we must have in our lives when we are standing in faith. Never dwell in the darkness of despair. Come to Jesus in Faith and tell Him what you expect from Him. He will answer you!

How faith and forgiveness Helped Me Heal

I became acutely aware that forgiveness had to take place and was necessary for my healing and restoration. So I chose to forgive, although it was NOT received immediately. I also began to intercede on my mother's behalf, asking the Lord to reveal the truth to her. Through that process of fasting and praying, God began to infuse my heart with an overwhelming unconditional love for my mother in my heart.

Then, I began my nutrition program that included different holistic modalities. Before I took any nutritional supplements, I would anoint myself, pray over my supplements, and give them their assignment in my body!

After the 5th day, the number of GRACE, I began to have energy like I could run a marathon…and I KNEW then, God was up to something! On the 7th day, the number of DIVINE PERFECTION, I could no longer feel the huge lump there. Now it's November 8th, the number of NEW BEGINNINGS, and I wanted it confirmed and noted that GOD HAD WORKED A MIRACLE IN MY BODY IN 8 DAYS! So I went to a Screening Center and waited most of the day to have an Ultrasound done…and then!

It was CONFIRMED that there was NO EVIDENCE of that diagnosis eight days prior!

Through the power of prayer, forgiveness, whole food nutrition, I stand today free, healthy, whole, and "Healed Twice" IN JESUS' NAME.

And over time, the Lord completely RESTORED my mother's and my relationship, she took ill a few years later, and I was able to care for her until she breathed her last breath and made her transition in Nov 2013. To God, Be ALL THE GLORY!

God is a God of restoration. He is a God of healing. He brought deliverance to my life, both physically and emotionally. As we see so many times throughout the Scriptures, He is both willing and able to restore people's lives to a place of holistic well-being. There are countless stories in the gospels that tell us of Jesus reaching into the broken lives of others and making them new once more. That's what our Savior is all about.

God is both the author and sustainer of life. He shaped the world and everything in it, including us. So, He knows better than anyone what we need. That's why Jesus is often called "the great physician." He is the most incredible doctor we could ever receive treatment from, and we should also ensure that's He's at the head of our wellness plan. The healing and deliverance we will receive will ultimately come through faith, just as it has for so many people in the past.

He brought me from a place of brokenness to a place of profound healing, just like the woman in the story. I realized that all I had to do to receive His healing just like her was to seek Him. I had to let faith lead my life by the power of the Holy Spirit, and then I would be opened up to God's immeasurable healing presence in my life. I couldn't do it on my power alone, but by the strength and power that flowed through me as a child of God.

Never forget the profound Words of Philippians 4:13: "*I can do all things through Christ who strengthens me.*" When faced with a devasting crossroads in your life, we have one of two options: we can submit to the despair of the trial we are facing, or we can submit to our faith which will deliver us.

In the moment, it may be challenging. It may feel as if we don't truly have that choice, that we must submit to our despair. You must stand tall in God's mighty power. Forgiveness is one of the most effective ways to rid our bodies of the toxicity produced within us by harboring sinful resentment toward others. Remember that you can accomplish anything through Christ because He has won the victory over death and sin, and He shares that victory with you. So you CAN do all things through Christ who strengthens you.

I want to take a look at one of my favorite stories of healing in the gospels. It is the story of the leper, who is healed by the touch of Jesus. It is one of my favorites because it shows both the remarkable power of faith and the unexplainable compassion of our Lord.

We all experience illness at some point in our lives. Some are minor and simply annoying, while others can be catastrophic and life-threatening. Illness is a major contender in our lives. It disrupts our everyday life and steals those we love from us. Illness is an enemy that we must fight at all costs.

Illness is such a struggle because it is antithetical to everything that God is. God is the very definition of life and love. He not only made everything in the world and gave it life, but He also continually sustains that life. He also gave us the blessing of being able to bring new life into the world ourselves.

Illness steals life from us. It drains us of our energy and compromises our well-being. This is completely the opposite of everything God is. As His children, it's part of our mission to fight illness in this world. One way that we do that is by pursuing a deeper connection with Jesus. He is the great healer. He alone can purge us of whatever ails us. As we see throughout the Gospels, Jesus uses the power of God to bring healing to people's lives in every way.

Mark 1:40-45 gives us a beautiful illustration of this:
A man with leprosy came and knelt in front of Jesus, begging to be healed. "If you are willing, you can heal me and make me clean," he said. Moved with compassion, Jesus reached out and touched him. "I am willing," He said. "Be healed!" Instantly the leprosy disappeared, and the man was healed. Then Jesus sent him on his way with a stern warning: "Don't tell anyone about this. Instead, go to the priest and let him examine you. Take along the offering required in the law of Moses for those who have been healed of leprosy. This will be a public testimony that you have been cleansed." But the man went and spread the Word, proclaiming to everyone what had happened. As a result, large crowds soon surrounded Jesus, and He couldn't publicly enter a town anywhere. He had to stay out in the secluded places, but people from everywhere kept coming to Him.

While it may seem like a simple story of healing on the surface, it is actually so much more than that. Jesus heals the man of so much more than his leprosy. To understand how this is so, we must take a quick look into the culture and context of the times. When we do, it will peel back another layer of truth in this story.

Leprosy was a terrifying disease with no cure. Coming down with leprosy was pretty much a death sentence in the ancient world. Once you contracted it, you would develop excruciating sores that would spread all over your body. Your skin would become scaly and start to peel off. This condition would get so bad and become so painful that lepers would have to drag themselves along the ground because they no longer had the strength to stand. It was a slow, painful death.

Leprosy was thought to be highly contagious, and thus the leper was feared by the masses. When the priests inspected someone with leprosy and deemed them "unclean," they were banished from society. They lost all of their families, friends, and loved ones. Their families mourned them as if they were dead.

So, the leper would have already lost his health, his family, and his dignity. He had nothing left. He was humiliated and shamed by passerby's who feared him, mocked him, and ridiculed him. He was literally left to die, alone and without aid. While he was in the darkest depths of his despair, he likely heard of the Messiah and the incredible healing that was taking place in nearby towns. Suddenly, upon learning about Jesus, the leper was once again filled with hope.

He believed in Jesus so much that he threw himself at Jesus' feet, proclaiming Faith that Jesus could heal him. And that's exactly what Jesus did. But the way Jesus healed him was remarkable. Many times, when Jesus healed people, He did it simply with His Words. But Jesus chooses to touch the leper to heal him. This is significant because the leper had been robbed of the dignity of human touch. Jesus showed the leper that he was so valuable to Jesus that He was willing to touch him despite his disease. This brought healing to the leper not only physically but also mentally, emotionally, and spiritually.

When God's Healing looks different than What we Prayed

Your relationship with Jesus brings healing in so many ways! Jesus wants to bring you healing physically, mentally, emotionally, and spiritually. He wants to take all the hurt and pain you have experienced and bring unparalleled healing to your heart and body. No matter what you have experienced, a relationship with Jesus can bring unbelievable healing to you in every way. Countless believers throughout history have experienced His power in their lives, and it's available to you too. I would be remiss if I didn't mention the other piece to this reality; that is, He may not always choose to heal us on this side of Heaven. However, when we decide to stand firm in faith even when nothing changes, that's the ultimate proof of our devotion.

I encourage you to read all of 1 Corinthians 15, which states that our new spiritual body will be immortal and imperishable from our earthly body, free from disease, aging, and death. It will be free from sin and no longer subject to temptation. Along with that truth is God's Sovereignty found in Job 42:1-6, where we read how Job Worships God by acknowledging His Sovereignty. There are also Biblical reasons that God may not heal: Unconfessed sin, Lack of Faith, Failure to ask, Need for deliverance, and God's Timing.

The Necessity and Power of Forgiveness

As I found out in my life, unforgiveness and emotional distress can lead to frightening effects on our bodies. The following quote is from John Hopkins Hospital: *"Emotional stress can undermine your health, potentially impacting high blood pressure, susceptibility to illness, abuse of drugs or alcohol, less able to fight disease, and increasing the likelihood of depression"* (Stress | Johns Hopkins Medicine). That is just a snippet of the research that has shown the connection between our emotional and physical health.

We truly are holistic beings. Genesis 2:7 says, *"And the LORD God formed man of the dust of the ground and breathed into his nostrils the breath of life; and man became a living being."* In this verse, the Hebrew Word (the original language of the Old Testament) for "being" is שֶׁפֶנ or *nefesh*. This Word is typically translated as "being," but its meaning goes much deeper than that.

Nefesh, in and of itself, describes what a "living being" is. As the case with many Hebrew Words, *nefesh* contains within itself layers of meaning. There is a depth to this Word that draws out God's design for what it means to be a living being created in His image. *Nefesh* carries the idea of self, soul, mind, life, emotion, passion, will, and character. This verse is not just trying to express that humans are living, physical beings. This Word truly encompasses the holistic nature of what it means to be a living person made in the image of God.

This is further evidenced by the fact that *nefesh* isn't used in the Old Testament for other living things, such as plants that are living but have no sentient will or emotional capacity. *Nefesh* gives us biblical evidence of God's design that our emotional health is deeply connected to our physical beings. This is where the power of forgiveness comes in and provides us with our greatest weapon against emotional distress and unwellness.

Consider for a moment this way of thinking about sin. Perhaps sin is not just a particular action one does in a given situation, but rather its own existential force that influences people to make these kinds of decisions in their lives. Ephesians 6:10-13 says, *"Finally, my brethren, be strong in the Lord and in the power of His might. Put on the whole armor of God, that you may be able to stand against the wiles of the devil. For we do not wrestle against flesh and blood, but against principalities, against powers, against the rulers of the darkness of this age, against spiritual hosts of wickedness in the heavenly places. Therefore, take up the whole armor of God, that you may be able to withstand in the evil day, and having done all, to stand."*

We know that sin causes death, decay, and emotional distress within our lives. This is the agenda of the enemy. The "greatest" weapon we have to fight against evil is the Word of God (aka The Sword of the Spirit), which is why Jesus quoted Scripture in response to each of the temptations offered by Satan in the wilderness.

The need for forgiveness arises when injustice or sin is perpetrated against us. This is the influence of the enemy. Forgiveness is so powerful because when we exercise it, we look that evil in the face and deny its power over us. We choose to look past the sinful influences that affect the other person, seeing through to the goodness and the image of God that they carry within themselves. In doing so, we are cutting off the power of Satan over our lives and choosing instead to submit to God's goodness, which will prevail every time.

Our Savior, Jesus Christ, demonstrated this most remarkably. He took on the fullness of the ultimate evil, death. Death is the ultimate evil because it is the antithesis of everything that God is. But Jesus looked it straight in the face, denied its power over Him, and rose from the grave. That victory secured the eternal salvation of all of us who call on His name. Through that victory, He shares with all the miraculous healing power of forgiveness that He showed towards each one of us as He took on our sins on the cross.

So, when you forgive another, you bring healing to both of you. You are freeing them from the burden of their sin while also freeing yourself from the emotional and physical burden of the sin forged against you. This is a necessary action if you are to walk through the Christian life. In Matthew 6:14-15, Jesus makes clear how serious He takes the matter of forgiveness: *"For if you forgive men their trespasses, your heavenly Father will also forgive you. But if you do not forgive men their trespasses, neither will your Father forgive your trespasses."*

If you don't extend forgiveness, you will find out just how devastating the physiological burdens of unforgiveness and emotional distress can be. This is what I experienced. I held on to my pain and then faced a diagnosis that could have drastically altered, if not ended, my life. The effects of unforgiveness are no joke. This is precisely what Paul is talking about when he writes, *"For the wages of sin is death, but the gift of God is eternal life in Christ Jesus our Lord"* (Romans 6:23).

In Luke 7:47, Jesus teaches a profound lesson: *"Therefore I say to you, her sins, which are many, are forgiven, for she loved much. But to whom little is forgiven, the same loves little."* Forgiveness is tied directly to love! And we know that as children of God, our mission in life is to embody and spread the love of Jesus. This means that not only does our aptitude for forgiveness determine our physical and emotional health, but our spiritual wellness too! How can we possibly draw close to Jesus if we don't live out the traits that define His very existence?

In Matthew 26:28, Jesus says, *"For this is My blood of the new covenant, which is shed for many for the forgiveness of sins."* Never forget that Jesus' own blood was spilled for the sake of forgiveness. He went through the torturous agony that He did so that He could extend forgiveness to every one of us. He led by example, and He calls us to follow. As I found out the hard way, responding to His call can easily save your life.

When you face your greatest trials in life, remember to embrace God's Love, perfect your love walk, and breakthrough rather than break down. He will help you to rise above anything you may face. You can trust in Him completely. God is a God of healing, and His deliverance knows no bounds. I was healed twice through Faith in Jesus, both emotionally and then physically. I know you can too. May God Bless You with His Choice Blessing!

Why Forgiveness is Essential

To receive a harvest of any kind, you must first plant a seed. God, Himself started with a seed, His only begotten son, Jesus. The first chapter of John refers to Jesus as the Word. "In the beginning was the Word, and the Word was with God, and the Word was God." A Seed does not get activated until it is planted. In this chapter, the soil for your planted seed, which is God's Word, will be your heart.

In Mark the 4th chapter, Jesus refers to the planting of natural seeds being the same as spiritual truths in the heart. When we have the right conditions, a natural seed can be planted and bear much fruit the same way the Word of God can.

You must ask yourself which seeds have been planted in your heart?
Good seeds, such as the Word of God, that can produce healing? Seeds of hope, love, support, edification? Or, bad ones like discord, betrayal, lies, abuse, emotional trauma, or deception can choke out the good ones.

How is a life-giving seed planted in the heart?
By the Word of God, it produces after its own kind. The Word of God is life; therefore, that's what it produces.

In Mark 4:1, Jesus begins to teach again, building up their faith. Faith comes by hearing; He wanted them to know how to receive and not just be healed, and this was a spiritual truth. As you listen to the Word of God on healing, that healing seed gets planted.

The condition of your soil (heart) matters.

A healthy harvest can not grow if the soil (heart) is hard, dry, and cracked—Harboring hatred, unforgiveness, bitterness, or rath. When you choose to forgive, that causes your soil (heart) to become softened and nutrient-dense ready to receive seeds that will produce the kind of harvest you desire.

We must deal with these human hearts and let our spirit man lead us.

Scripture says: Jeremiah 17:9-10 The Living Bible (TLB)
9-10 [9] The heart is the most deceitful thing there is and desperately wicked. No one can really know how bad it is! [10] Only the Lord knows! He searches all hearts and examines deepest motives so he can give to each person his right reward, according to his deeds—how he has lived.
Everyone should always ask themselves if the apologies you've offered, the same depth and sincerity of the type that's acceptable to you.

We should all be extenders of the same measure of grace that Christ has extended to us.

Matthew 5:22-24 The Message:

21-22 "You're familiar with the command to the ancients, 'Do not murder.' I'm telling you that anyone who is so much as angry with a brother or sister is guilty of murder. Carelessly call a brother 'idiot!' and you just might find yourself hauled into court. Thoughtlessly yell 'stupid!' at a sister, and you are on the brink of hellfire. The simple moral fact is that Words kill.

23-24 "This is how I want you to conduct yourself in these matters. If you enter your place of worship and, about to make an offering, you suddenly remember a grudge a friend has against you, abandon your offering, leave immediately, go to this friend and make things right. Then and only then, come back and work things out with God.

We have to deal with these human hearts and let our spirit man lead us.

I KNOW these scriptures can be tough to walk out in the middle of chaos and heartbreak for some. But, I promise you, this is precisely what allowed me to receive my physical and emotional healing. The key to opening your imprisoned heart is to surrender and make a choice, so YOU can be free and made whole.

When you surrender entirely, you will no longer feel the same weight and struggle you did from the resistance of it.

When you choose not to forgive or find it difficult, your heart functions like a prison cell that holds that person hostage in your heart like a trapped prisoner. You won't release them because you haven't found or used the necessary keys. So, you carry them around; they lie down with you, they get up with you. Their where ever you are until the prison doors are opened, and they are released from you.

As I end this sub-chapter, look at unforgiveness in this way. Those you don't forgive are given greater access to your heart than God has.

Mark 11:22-26 is mentioned throughout this book, but what's really interesting is that all Bible translations don't include verse 26! They have it as a footnote. This is HUGE, sisters; this shows that God's forgiveness towards us is conditional. If you don't forgive, He won't forgive; don't miss this.

Seedtime and Harvest

The Word of God is a seed that possesses everything needed to produce the healing you need for your soul, body, and spirit. It has the potential to bring a harvest of healing if given the right fertile soil. Many things can occur in life that cause a part of us to die. However, as women of faith, I want to remind you that the Resurrection is NOT only an event; the Resurrection is a person; name Jesus as well!

He desires to resurrect some of those dead things in our lives, such as dreams, hopes, desires and love that some situations have killed.

Give Him access.

Beauty Reflections:

What did you discover about yourself?
What action will you take?

He has made everything Beautiful in its time. Ecclesiastes 3:11

_____

_____

_____

_____

_____

_____

_____

_____

_____

_____

_____

All Things Beautiful

Chapter 2

FAITH

Finding Your Identity

What does it mean to be a believer? What do you believe in, or who do you believe? It's amazing that although people can believe in many things, generally, when you hear the word "believer," Christian comes to mind. That's the power of this title!

How did it come about? By the early church, who first believed in Jesus as the Son of God, the Christ.

So, when people are called believers, they believe in Christ. No argument! However, what does believing in Christ entail? This is the question that, when answered correctly, will turn your life around. Three principal elements mark the life of a believer of Christ. They are love, faith, and hope, according to 1 Corinthians 13:13. These are the basis for walking with God, and they're proven signs you find all through the scriptures in the lives of those who walked with God.

God is love. Faith is the condition that allows you to walk with God. Hope is the expectation of receiving all that God is and all He has promised you, and it is validated through faith. Let's talk about faith.

Faith is the principal factor when coming to God and even in walking with Him after you've come to Him. As a believing sister, your whole life is open to the possibilities your faith allows it to receive.

<u>Faith Is Your Key</u>

There's a revelation the bible gives in the book of *Hebrews 11:6 ESV. It says:*
"And without faith it is impossible to please Him, for whoever would draw near to God must believe that he exists and that He rewards those who seek Him."

In other words, she who comes to God must believe that He exists and that He will reward her for seeking Him tirelessly. Faith is the principal key to walking with God. It opens all other doors to receiving from God. By faith, you have blessings, love, hope, and every other promise from God.

It is noteworthy that the writer tries to capture a simplistic but powerful definition of faith earlier in this chapter. He says in Hebrews 11:1 ESV;

"Now faith is the assurance of things hoped for, the conviction of things not seen."

Faith is the assurance. It's a feeling, but more than just a feeling; it is assurance!

A sister who has faith in God is convinced beyond every doubt on every matter she believes in God for. This strengthens the resolve to seek God in multi-dimensions diligently.

Her faith is the driving force that keeps her going, seeking God tirelessly. It's the evidence that seals her as a true believer because every believer must have faith in God. Her faith is like mount Zion that cannot be moved. When she sets out to ask God for something, she stays there in that secret place until God shows up with answers.

It's by faith that the woman of God finds her identity in Christ. Yes, finding your identity and living it out is a process; it starts with faith, is sustained by faith and ends with faith. There's a transforming process every believer must go through, and sister, you must go through it as well.

The bible says in 2 Corinthians 3:18 ESV;
"And we all, with unveiled face, beholding the glory of the Lord, are being transformed into the same image from one degree of glory to another. For this comes from the Lord who is the Spirit."

So, from this revelation, you can be transformed into the glorious image of Christ seated in heaven. It is a gradual process that seeks your indulgence, and this means coming into the reality of your identity in Christ is a process that must be carefully and intentionally engaged.

You're not just a young lady or young woman, or whatever your preference is. You're more than you think you should be. There's a level of life that's available for you to live, if only you're willing.

How To Come Into Your Identity

Some blessings are given by default, but some, you have to work out your salvation with fear and trembling. Philippians 2:12.

In Christ, there are blessings, but some come with your participation. If God has given all these to you, then you'd love to know how to obtain them, right?

In God's system, it is not totally up to Him, neither is it totally up to you. It's always a system of joint efforts; God stretches out His arm to give, and you stretch out yours to receive. You need to understand the strategies to adopt in receiving from God. You have been given by grace, but seeing them in your life is not automatic. These blessings and your identity are in heavenly places and must be worked out into this earth realm, and this is where some get it wrong. You have to actively participate; that's faith!

Here are some things to do in establishing your identity:

1. Receive Christ
If you want to become like Christ and become all that He is, then it's only logical to first receive the truth of His person and Lordship. This is a step that should not be undermined. There's a confession of faith that grants your first step into the actualization of Christ's identity becoming yours. It's not enough to have been going to church for ages. There must be that moment when you intentionally decide to surrender to Jesus, and this is done by faith.

It says in Romans 10:9-10 ESV

"Because, if you confess with your mouth that Jesus is Lord and believe in your heart that God raised him from the dead, you will be saved. For with the heart one believes and is justified, and with the mouth one confesses and is saved."

You believe in your heart, and then you confess with your mouth unashamedly that Jesus is your Lord. This is the first step!

2. Becoming Through Prayer

Prayer is such a valuable and formidable instrument. In the place of prayer, there are limitless possibilities. It was in the place of prayer that Moses' face was transformed to shine. *Exodus 34:29.*

It was also in the place of prayer that Jesus was transfigured. Matthew 17:2.

This reveals that prayer can change the identity of a person spiritually as well as physically. Prayer is not only a place of asking from God, but also a place of contact with God. The moment you begin speaking with God, you have entered the prayer realm. Practice this every day and make it a part of you. You don't have to find a quiet place or a secret place. That's important, but you must look beyond the former limitations and know that now God is in you. You can talk to Him every time and everywhere.

3. Becoming Through knowledge

Knowledge of the Word of God is the knowledge to become like God. God has revealed everything about Himself through his Word, the Bible. You need to study this book of his Word diligently and fully focused on faith. Don't just read it like a compendium of bedtime stories. They are the revelation of obtainable possibilities. The bible says that they have all been recorded for our good.

It says in Romans 15:4 ESV;
"For whatever was written in former days was written for our instruction, that through endurance and through the encouragement of the Scriptures, we might have hope."

The Word of God can inform you of who you are supposed to be in Christ. Just as Jesus knew what was written about Him and it was a great advantage to the completion of his earthly ministry.

4. Becoming Through Fellowship
As hinted earlier, prayer is not only a place to bombard God with your requests. It is also the place of fellowship. It's where you meet God and touch eternity which transfers his reality to become your reality. In the place of prayer, your mind is transformed into the mind of Christ. In the place of prayer, the Holy Spirit who is in you can open you up to what God wants you to receive.

The bible says in Isaiah 40:31 ESV;
"But they who wait for the LORD shall renew their strength; they shall mount up with wings like eagles; they shall run and not be weary; they shall walk and not faint."
Waiting is done in the place of prayer, which is the place of fellowship. It is a law that you gradually become what you focus on. When you make time for quality fellowship and worship of God, you will keep transforming and becoming like Him. In the place of fellowship, your strength is renewed;

you gain strength beyond your ability; you receive the nature of God that does not faint and does not experience weariness; you become a spiritual giant and a force that men reckon with in this physical realm as well.

Faith is the principal ingredient that validates all of these actions. There are blessings that God has given you, which are for life and godliness, meaning they affect every sphere of your life.

In your identity in Christ are both spiritual advantages and physical advantages. You are a favored woman according to God's eternal counsel, and He only awaits your coming into this reality that is set before you.

Know Who You Are In Christ

"When the purpose is not known, abuse is inevitable." This is a popular sentence you might have heard several times now, and the late Dr. Myles Munroe said it, and he got it spot on.

Abuse of anything is only a matter of time if it is not clearly defined. If its parameters are not well explained and understood, there's the likelihood of overusing or underusing it. This is not only true for inanimate objects and inventions of man. If you fail to understand your design and a new identity in Christ, you will also fall victim to this tragedy. Don't be where God has not put you. Don't do things that God has not planned for you to do. Don't undermine the potentials in you by identity misinformation.

You need to know who you are. You are a renewed spirit that has been given potential beyond your comprehension. Finding potential is tied to your hunger for it, and it takes you searching and being willing to commune with Christ, the initiator of this life you seek to know.

You could easily settle for less when you're not aware of how great you are. There's so much that God has put in you. The presence of the Holy Spirit in you is access to a limitless supply that you should be harnessing. Don't let lack of knowledge make you settle for less than you're worth in any way. You're a woman of wisdom, power, and a sound mind. There are blessings and riches with your name on them, all lined up for your taking. So, are you going to take them or what? If you don't take them, you will not attain levels that you should have because you thought you couldn't.

Understanding your identity in Christ and walking in the knowledge of it will save you the stress you're going through right now because of ignorance. It's really, as God said in Hosea 4:6, that people can perish because of ignorance. Notice that God also said in *Hosea 4:6, "My people are destroyed for lack of knowledge…"*. God is talking about "His" people. So, being a "Christian" is not all there is to this journey. There's also the aspect of obtaining knowledge that will practically lift you into a realm of life that you formerly didn't experience or even know was possible. There are great possibilities in this kingdom that only come to those who find their identity in Christ.

Who Does God Say That YOU Are?

Let's explore that, but before we do, I have another question.

Why does what others say to you and about you hurt, but what God says about you DOES NOT excite you?

Ponder that...

The one that formed you says these things about you.

Friend

Jesus calls you his friend: John 15:14-15 ESV;
"You are my friends if you do what I command you. No longer do I call you servants, for the servant, does not know what his master is doing, but I have called you friends, for all that I have heard from my Father I have made known to you."

Sister

You are his sister. That's another level of relationship: *John 20:17 GW.;*
'Jesus told her, "Don't hold on to me. I have not yet gone to the Father. But go to my brothers and sisters and tell them, 'I am going to my Father and your Father, to my God and your God.'"'

Blessed

You have been blessed above what you think and know: *Ephesians 1:3 ESV;*
"Blessed be the God and Father of our Lord Jesus Christ, who has blessed us in Christ with every spiritual blessing in the heavenly places."

Victorious

You have received the victory that is in Christ. This victory is for you when you walk in step with God: *1 John 5:4 ESV;*
"For everyone who has been born of God overcomes the world. And this is the victory that has overcome the world— our faith. Who is it that overcomes the world except the one who believes that Jesus is the Son of God?"

Saved

You have no fears when you believe in God and walk with God. You are saved through Christ. Among other things, eternal life also contains salvation: *John 6:47 ESV;*
"Truly, truly, I say to you, whoever believes has eternal life."

Righteous

You are the righteousness of God in Christ Jesus. This is a gift you have received: *2 Corinthians 5:21*
"For our sake He made Him to be sin who knew no sin, so that in Him we might become the righteousness of God."

Sanctified and Justified

Sanctification means acceptance; justification means being free from any accusation: *1 Corinthians 6:11 ESV; "And such were some of you. But you were washed, you were sanctified, you were justified in the name of the Lord Jesus Christ and by the Spirit of our God."* These are but a few to mention of what God has given you.

Beauty Reflections:

What did you discover about yourself?
What action will you take?

He has made everything Beautiful in its time. Ecclesiastes 3:11

Chapter 3

Self-Care

Balance

My dear sisters, balance is one of the most important things God gave creation; it's all about time. There's a balance for the earth as the sun rises and men go to work, that it should also set, and men would rest. As the time for birth is a time to add to the earth, death also comes to take from the earth. There's also planting and harvesting and many more things that portray the law of God's Balance. These are all systems God put in and around your life to give you the wisdom to create balance in your life.

Many times, the bible teaches that all things should be done in "moderation."

It says in Ecclesiastes. 3:1 ESV:
"For everything, there is a season and a time for every matter under heaven."

Every matter under heaven should have its proper time allocated to it.

As a lady, there's already pressure to work as hard as possible to achieve and build something for yourself. There's definitely dignity in labor, but it must be done in the right manner. You can't work all the time. There's a need to work, but don't get swallowed up in your "hustle." This is the most common side of the pendulum to swing to. Some ladies may get too lazy and allow leisure time to interfere with work, but this is rarely the case.

In all, you have to do in your world, and all you have to be, moderation is the key. You need to strike a wise balance between what you want to achieve in your career and your life outside of your career.

Some people need your attention now. If you build the notion that you need to achieve things before you make time for people who matter to you, it's a risky bet. Not everyone gets that kind of opportunity. Many people lose out on good friends, relationships, family, and variations of the better things of life in the pursuit of a career and a name, only to get burnt at the end of the day. Hey, sis, what about your wellbeing? What time do you make for yourself? Or do you even know how important you are? It wouldn't be your life without you in it. Think about that!

So, here are calculated steps to take as you power through life, making the best of everything:

1. Make Time For Yourself
If you don't give yourself time to recalibrate and refresh, you'll be performing below average. Learn to set aside time for yourself. Take a few moments to yourself every day or each week, and do some fun stuff for "you". Enjoy life. Take stock of what's working for you and what's not. That's how to make progress.

2. Make Time For Your Relationships

Your relationships are meaningful. It may look like a distraction to work on them, but that's not always the case. I'm not saying there aren't relationships that sap the life out of you. However, if yours isn't, then it's worth the time. If it's a promising relationship, why not put in the time, right? Do your best to water it with time and attention to make it grow properly. Create a healthy balance between your relationship and work life. Don't let one side cause problems for the other.

3. Make Time For Friends

Yes, you need to make separate time for yourself, your relationship, and your friends. Why? Because the bond with friends is just totally different. When you're with friends, you may not have time to think about your plans, goals, and whatever else. Time for friends is usually time for fun with "others." Don't neglect friends in the name of work. As much as they're your fun tribe, they're also your most solid support system. When relationships end or you lose a job, friends are the ones who still hang around. You must invest in these people. Don't let work-life rob you of their love and contribution to your life.

4. Leave Work At Work

Something that could make your life complex and muffled up is taking work home. What I mean is when you're done with work or office hours, leave it at that. If there's more work, let it roll over to the next working day. Work drains your energy. Even if you work from home or work for yourself, try to make "time boundaries," after which you'd stop all forms of work and just relax. When you get too indulged in work, you begin to get cranky. You lose vital time you should use for other things because work never finishes!

5. Leave Leisure Outside Of Work

Another wrong move is trying to take "comfort" or regular life affairs into the workspace. Meaning, you can't mix work time with leisure time. This is one of the things that can get you doing overtime. Over time, in turn, takes away the free time you should have had. This will always cause a mix-up and disorient your planned Balance.

Balance is all about calculation and intention, and it doesn't come automatically; you make a choice that enforces it. Now, the question is, "Do you think you need to balance things out?" How are the scales tipped in your work/life balance?

Mental Health

Mental health has become a more popular topic in recent years, and it has drawn the attention of the whole world, and the World Health Organization is particular about it.

In the dictionary, the definition of mental health is the condition of a person's emotional well-being, especially concerning one's outlook on life, ability to cope with stress or the absence of a mental disorder. This is as defined by the Advanced English Dictionary.

A woman's mental health can be disturbed by depression and anxiety, among other disorders. These have made an impact that's still being fought desperately.

Depression affects men but seems to have more numbers

among women, according to reports. Clinical depression is a serious and pervasive mood disorder that causes hopelessness, sadness, helplessness and worthlessness. It makes you feel like you're not good and have nothing good to offer. Women must deal with this stealer of peace and sound mind.

Your mental health is a cumulative total of everything that should affect your mental capacity. That means your mental health affects your whole being in essence. Your mental power is the ability to coordinate the various aspects of your life correctly and suitably for you. When mental health begins to fail a person, they lose the most vital parts that make up the human experience, such as making well-informed decisions, enjoying the good things around them, and many other devastating effects. These are the evils depression and anxiety cause.

Some symptoms of depression in women include:
- Little appetite
- Difficulty sleeping or too much sleep
- Sad mood, anxious mood, or empty mood
- Low self-esteem
- Loss of interest or pleasure in activities
- Feelings of guilt
- Suicidal thoughts
- Trouble concentrating, remembering or making decisions
- Physical symptoms such as headaches, digestive disorders, chronic pain, etc., not responding to treatment.

If you feel you have experiences with one or more of these, you can still overcome them. There are a few instructions that will help anyone who finds themselves in this devilish pit of depression. And even if you aren't, learn how to avoid it and protect your mental health.

1. Think Better Thoughts

This should be your first strategy to avoid depression or to come out of it. Most of the symptoms are observably having to do with the thought processes. Your mind is where a lot happens. It's the control tower of your body. When your mind is right, and thinking right, the body enjoys peace and prosperity. However, if otherwise, the body suffers and everything along with it.

This is what the bible says in *Proverbs 4:23 NKJV:*
"Keep your heart with all diligence, For out of it spring the issues of life."

If you're not keeping your heart vigilantly and you're letting every manner of thought not rooted in the Word of God flow into it, that could be a problem.

2. Seek God's Restoration

If you think you're prone to depression or you're already experiencing it, fear not. There's nothing the power of God is restricted to. It doesn't matter how it came or who brought it. God can override it. He can lift depression and anxiety or any other kind of mental health challenge. It's part of the grace God gives his children; His saving power.

The book of *Isaiah 26:3 Modern English Version 3 You will keep him in perfect peace, whose mind is stayed on You, because he trusts in You.*

Could it be you stopped trusting God and let these transgressing thoughts take control of your mind? It could be. Depression comes majorly from worrisome thoughts that you can't control.

Pray to God about it. Seek his hand of restoration over your life. As much as depression has medical explanations, it can also be escalated by demonic spirits who take an opportunity where they find one. Therefore, you need the power of God to liberate your mind and make you whole again.

3. Get Medical Help
There are medical systems for treating these conditions. They should be indulged prayerfully as the need for divine intervention is always an advantage. Prescribed treatments can help women overcome this challenge.

Your mental health comprises many things put in the right place. Keep these great factors in mind: guided thoughts and proper rest. Do you feel depressed? Are you paying attention to your mental health?

Celebrating Your Wins

A good win makes the heart merry. At one point, every person deserves a win.

So, if you're getting your wins, that's a thumbs up, but do you celebrate them?

Celebrations don't have to be ungodly, not at all. What do

you think the Psalmist was teaching in many of the Psalms? There's so much to learn from the Psalms.

If you've made it this far, no matter how little you think that might be, it's still worth celebrating. If you believe you haven't achieved enough, well, guess what? Many who started this race with you are nowhere to be found today. When I say nowhere, I mean, not just that they gave up, they're actually not even alive today, but you still are.

There's so much to thank God for. So, next time, whether it's a small win, a big win, or no win, celebrate. Celebrate the grace of God in your life. Celebrate the ability to have attempted, and celebrate winning at your attempt!

One of the reasons some women don't celebrate is because they think they've not achieved enough yet. Don't let that kind of mindset be your motivation. You've got to thank God every time for everything, and you've got to celebrate more!

So, here's what to do:

1. Realize It Was God
You need to know that nothing has been done by your power alone; all that you have has been given to you by the Father. No matter how much you've had to put into it, everything you can do is given by God. The gift came from above, from God the heavenly Father.

The bible says in *James. 1:17 ESV:*
"Every good gift and every perfect gift is from above, coming down from the Father of lights, with whom there is no variation or shadow due to change."

You've got to be thankful that you have that gift that got you that win. This is why you need to be celebrating. Celebrating is an appreciation to God, more than a self-gratifying desire.

2. Be Contented
So, this is for those thinking it was probably too small a win to celebrate. Love what God has given you. Don't get distracted looking to the left and right, measuring what your colleagues achieved that looked better than yours. That's an attitude God doesn't condone because it does not bring Him any Glory. When God does something for you, you must learn to shut out the noise and pretend you didn't see anybody else having anything. You sincerely thank Him like He's never done it for anybody else. This doesn't mean to kick everybody else down. It's rather a mindset that gives God thanks for what He did for you, regardless of what He didn't do according to your limited knowledge.

The bible says in 1 Thessalonians. 5:18 ESV:
"Give thanks in all circumstances; for this is the will of God in Christ Jesus for you."

Sis, You've got to thank Him for everything, always.

3. Prepare To Go Bigger
In celebrating your "small" wins, God is setting you up for something bigger. Remember that the servant who uses the little talents or gifts to glorify the Master gets rewarded for it. It's not only when you work with what you were given that you get rewarded, by thanks as well, when you show you know what was given to you.

It's pride not to return thanks to God or belittle what good

God is doing in your life.

His Word says in *Matthew 25:29 ESV:*
"For to everyone who has will more be given, and he will have an abundance. But from the one who has not, even what he has will be taken away."

This is the meaning of this parable: She who has little will lose what she has because of ignorance concerning what has been given to her. If she doesn't celebrate what God has given her in a way that appreciates God, she's obstructing her elevation to the next level.

Knowing that celebrating your wins is what God wants is a good start to where you're going. Celebrating shouldn't take you out of the presence of God; no, it should keep you there.

The bible says in Psalm 100:4-5 ESV:
"Enter his gates with thanksgiving, and his courts with praise! Give thanks to Him; bless his name! For the LORD is good; his steadfast love endures forever, and his faithfulness to all generations."

Take your friends, go out, and celebrate. If the Lord lays it on your heart, share it. In all, always have a godly celebration to mark an achievement God has made through you as you prepare for your next level. Will you celebrate that "small" win today?

Beauty Reflections:

What did you discover about yourself?
What action will you take?

He has made everything Beautiful in its time. Ecclesiastes 3:11

_____

_____

_____

_____

_____

_____

_____

_____

_____

_____

_____

Chapter 4

Outward Beauty

Eyelashes

<u>Things Every Lash Wearer Need to Know</u>

If eyes are the windows to the soul, then eyelashes are the curtains that leave a good or bad impression on the viewer. In my humble opinion, eyelashes simply make your eyes sparkle!

We all have eyelashes to protect our eyes, not just to enhance our beauty. Our upper eyelids hold between 90 to 200 lashes, while the lower eyelids have about 70 to 100. On average, we shed 1-4 lashes every day.

Some women (and, very unfairly, many men) are blessed with naturally long and full eyelashes, but some are not so fortunate.

If you are not in the long-eyelash club, do not stress, there are natural ways to make them longer and more robust. Many different enhancing techniques will make your eyelashes long, thick, and absolutely gorgeous.

How to Make Your Lashes Grow Longer and Thicker

As I have mentioned earlier, not everyone is blessed with naturally long, full eyelashes. And some women damage their lashes by always wearing eyelash extensions or false eyelashes; aging can also affect them.

Whatever the case is, there are several natural ways to help your eyelashes out and make them healthier, thicker, and longer. You probably have most of my recommendations in your kitchen or medicine cabinet already, which is always a big plus for D.I.Y. remedy lovers.

Use Castor oil.
There is a lot of information about cold-pressed castor oil's ability to improve your eyelashes' strength and length. This is what I use. Natural castor oil contains essential fatty acids that act as emollients, which means that they moisturize and soften your eyelashes. A straightforward way to apply castor oil is to start with clean hands, dab a small amount on your fingertip, run along the lash line before going to bed. Upon waking, remove the castor oil with a make-up remover wipe.

Don't Use Eyelash Enhancements Without Proper Care of Your Eyelashes
One popular way to temporarily increase the length of your eyelashes is to get eyelash extensions. Eyelash extensions can look great; we can all agree on that. However, it is worth noting that the glue used in the application process can damage your natural eyelashes and leave them weak with

excessive use without consistent care of your natural lash.

There is nothing wrong with reaching for false eyelashes; for the most part, I often wear them. You may only wear them if you're going to a party or other special events. But, if you notice that you are reaching for them more frequently, your eyelashes are going to become shorter, thinner, and uneven over time without the proper care for them.

Moisturize with Coconut Oil
Coconut oil is an excellent moisturizer and strengthener for your eyelashes, and it is safe for use around your eyes. Just like castor oil, you can rub a little bit into your fingers until it becomes liquid, and then massage it into your eyelashes.

Eat a Healthy, Balanced Diet
Eating a balanced diet full of essential nutrients can help you grow thicker, fuller, and more prominent hair, including your eyelashes. Eating healthy food is vital, but drinking plenty of water is necessary too. Staying hydrated will help you stay energetic and alert but it is also essential for healthy skin and hair, your eyelashes included.

Try an Eyelash Growth Serum.
You may be aware of many different eyelash growth serums that can boost the length of your lashes on your Instagram or Facebook timeline since all the beauty gurus are raving about it. The beauty industry has many different kinds of this growth serum, but that does not mean you should buy the first one you see. Make sure to check the ingredient list to find the safest and the best eyelash growth serums. As mentioned earlier, one of the oldest, most cost-efficient serums for growth is cold-pressed Castor Oil.

Different Types of Eyelash Enhancements

Strip lashes – False Eyelashes
Strip lashes are known to most as false eyelashes, and they are beloved by many women worldwide. They come in a strip (as the name suggests), and the strip is glued to your natural eyelashes and eyelash line. *Ladies, I must tell you, this is my favorite lash enhancement and the most affordable.* You can cut them into pieces to make the application much more manageable and seamless.

These lashes will take any make-up look to the next level, and will make it look more professional and more put-together. They will also hide all of the eyeliner and eyeshadow mistakes you might make in the process. I am so excited to market a patent-pending strip lash system that will give the end-user multiple options for greater ease.

Make sure you stay connected for all that is to come.

My advice is to avoid clear eyelash glue and always go for the black one because it will give your make-up an "eyeliner" look and not be noticeable.

Individual lashes
Individual eyelashes are groups of three or more synthetic, silk, or mink lashes attached to each other. They can be applied to your eyelid or eyelash using lash glue; I prefer rubber-like glue (not hair glue) because it's pliable and doesn't dry hard. This technique will last up to two weeks.

Individual eyelashes are great because they offer you the option of choice: when you open the pack, you can pick the eyelashes based on the style you want for your eyelashes. You can even apply individual eyelashes in the areas that you feel are naturally lacking.

The application process is around 30 minutes, or less and this option of eyelash enhancement is very budget-friendly.

Magnetic lashes
Magnetic lashes are a new make-up trend becoming the latest craze in the beauty and make-up world.

Magnetic lashes are a new, simple way to attach false lashes without any glue and for a fraction of the time. Magnetic lashes are very cost-effective (because they can be reused dozens of times), hassle-free and mess-free way to have long, beautiful, luscious lashes.

Magnetic lashes come with a magnetic liner applied on the eyelid, and they just magnetically stick to it. The downside is they can not be worn during M.R.I. testing. The other downside to magnetic lashes is that if you do not put on enough magnetic liner, they can lift and even fly away on a windy day. Also, note that iron oxide, which causes the liner to be magnetic, can stain your skin; these lashes should be removed daily.

Eyelash Extensions
Eyelash extensions are the most costly of all the enhancements listed; they are semi-permanent eyelashes glued on your natural lashes by a lash technician. The process itself is much less intense than it sounds. Because eyelash extensions are

glued on individually, they are customizable, take up to two hours to apply, look much more natural, and are a long-term solution.

The eyelash glue for this technique is the strongest of them all. Therefore, it is vital to have lashes applied by a skilled technician so temporary or permanent damage doesn't occur, such as madarosis, which is caused by any process that damages the hair bulb or hair shaft, leading to either temporary or permanent hair loss. Common causes of madarosis include Staphylococcal infection—herpes simplex and even some dermatological disorders to complex systemic diseases.

Lash extensions can last close to six to eight weeks if you take good care of them. A downside to this technique is, they are attaching one single extension hair to one of your natural lashes. As stated above, we shed 1-4 lashes every day, so with the eyelash life cycle consisting of three phases, your look will change from natural fall out. At this point, the new lash will start to emerge and will take time to grow before you can affix another lash to it. If our lashes were on the same cycle, they would all fall out at the same time…Yikes!

Once the glue gets too weak to hold them, they will fall out naturally, just like your natural lashes do. Save your eyes and eyelash health by always going to a professional who knows what they are doing!

Eyebrows

How To Determine Which Eyebrow Shape Suits Your Face Shape

The craze around eyebrows is not new; eyebrows are the frame of your face, and they can make or break your look, which is why they require special attention.

Eyebrows trends have been changing for decades, and the changes between styles were pretty drastic (remember Twiggy's eyebrows that were trendy in the '50s and Cybill Shepherd's eyebrows that were a trend in the '60s).

Who knows what the new eyebrow trend is going to be? However, keep in mind that trends come and go, but over-tweezing can never be reversed, and your eyebrows do not forgive, especially when you get older than twenty. So, before you go aggressive with the tweezers, try to first consider your face shape.

Your brow and face shapes should complement each other and work together as a whole, that is pleasing to the eye, yours and others.

Round face
If you have a round face shape, your eyebrows' sharp arches will provide a vertical point on your face. That will lift everything upwards rather than outwards. When you fill your eyebrows in, start at your arch and make it slightly darker than the rest of your brow. Avoid making your eyebrows look straight because it will make your face appear rounder.

Long Face

If you happen to have an elongated face, try to prolong your brows at the end and make them as long as possible without them ending up in your hairline. Stay away from short eyebrows, and never shave off the ends. If your eyebrow hairs are sparse at the ends, you should draw fill them in. This will play the trick on the eye, draw things horizontally, and balance out your features. The flat shape of an eyebrow will make your face appear more balanced.

Oval Face

If you have an oval face shape, consider yourself blessed. When it comes to this face shape, there are no rules. Everything looks good on this face shape. When you fill in your eyebrows, try to work with your face's dimensions for the most natural, flattering look.

Heart-shaped face

Since the focus of the heart-shaped face is already on the forehead and eyes, you would ideally want to keep things straight or rounded. Stay away from making your eyebrows too dark and heavy; they should not attract too much attention.

Square face

If you have a square face, your eyebrows should be thick and have a strong arch. A thicker, stronger color and shape of the eyebrow will balance out a heavier and more pronounced jawline. If your eyebrows are angled, that will help balance the face's squareness, so focus on your arch when shading in your eyebrows.

Tips And Tricks You Need To Know Regarding Eyebrows.
The eyebrow world is not easy to navigate, and there are definitely some tricks of the trade that can be learned in a more challenging or more straightforward way.

Many women learn these tricks way too late after making numerous mistakes along the way. To make this journey more straightforward and less bumpy, I have prepared all of the tricks needed – keep them in your pocket and use them as you need them, but they will change your life and eyebrow routine.

Exfoliate the skin under your eyebrows.
We need to exfoliate our skin to remove old dead skin cells that are very well-known to most of us. But often, when exfoliating the face of our skin, we forget that we have skin under our eyebrows too. Clogged pores under your eyebrow hair can stunt hair growth and cause blackheads and pimples. You should exfoliate the skin under your eyebrows at least twice per month, but please make sure to do so gently, without ripping the hair out. You can use your usual exfoliation product of choice and concentrate on that area, or you can make a sugar scrub at home, mixing white sugar with coconut oil. Make sure you wash it out using warm water and gentle motions.

Use oils to stimulate hair growth.
After you take off your make-up, you should gently massage your eyebrows for at least a minute with castor oil, almond oil, or olive oil and leave it on your eyebrows overnight. Any of these oils will help your eyebrows stronger and thicker by increasing circulation and stimulating cellular metabolism.

Give up perfection.
Perfect symmetry is not something you should ever strive for when it comes to your eyebrows' shape. Trying to make your eyebrows completely identical often ends in extreme over-plucking and ruining what you naturally have.

Remember, eyebrows are sisters, not twins.

Your eyebrows do not have to be thick to be beautiful.
The slim and elegant eyebrows are just as beautiful and elegant as thick ones; don't let anyone tell you different. So, if you don't have naturally thick eyebrows, don't push it and paint them in excess. Enhancing your natural features is always a better choice than painting on the parts you do not have.

Different eyebrow make-up options and which is the best for you
Many brow grooming options are available on the market, and picking the perfect one can be seriously stress-inducing. Some of the options available are powder, a pomade, pencils, soap eyebrows... How are you supposed to choose between all of these options when all you want is your eyebrows to be filled in?

Take it from me, someone who has tried every product under the sun. Some products are a hit, some are a miss, but every product will find its perfect market. The trick is finding your ideal eyebrow product match. But no worries, I am here to give you some advice and point you in the right direction.

Eyebrow Pencil

The pencil is the most popular eyebrow grooming product, and it is the key to adding a natural-looking definition to arches. Eyebrow pencils make for an excellent base for brow powder (which we will touch on later). You should reach for an eyebrow pencil if you have asymmetric eyebrows, bigger gaps between the hair, and sparse tails.

Using the pencil, draw short, feather-like strokes in the direction of your hair growth. Finish the brow by filling in your brows' inner corners with upward and outward hair-like strokes.

Eyebrow powder

If you aim for a softer, natural eyebrow look, this product is the perfect match for you.

Eyebrow powders fill in any sparse areas in the brows. On its own, eyebrow powder tends to have a softer effect than other products. Powder formulas also make eyebrows look fuller, and they help set brow pencils to make the make-up last longer.

You will need an angled brush to apply eyebrow powder; sweep it in the direction of your hair growth, but make sure you are using a light hand (you want eyebrows to look feathered). Make sure to use a spoolie brush to soften the edges and make them look more natural. If you do not have a spoolie, you can always use a cleaned mascara wand.

Eyebrow pomade

Eyebrow pomade gives brows a dramatic, defined look, giving brows a subtle hold. Eyebrow pomade is perfect for women with sparse or strong eyebrows because it helps you fake the bold eyebrow look, but it also allows you to enhance the eyebrows you have.

Dip a stiff, angled brush into the pomade and brush the pomade on with light, short strokes. Make sure you are beginning at the center of your brow and then forming your eyebrow from there. Use a spoolie to brush out the eyebrow hair, making them look more natural.

Eyebrow Enhancing Techniques
Some women have naturally thick and well-shaped eyebrows, but some are not as blessed. Aging, chemotherapy, medical conditions, and stress can all be reasons for sparse eyebrow hairs.

But, just like everything else in the world of beauty, there is a solution. Estheticians are offering different eyebrow enhancing techniques that can help with the appearance of your eyebrows. Some of the most popular ones are eyebrow lamination, ombre shading, and microblading.

Brow Lamination
Laminated eyebrows are a new eyebrow craze in the make-up world. Many models and celebrities are starting to wear full, almost "shiny" brows that appear to grow upwards.

This eyebrow enhancement originates from a beauty treatment called brow lamination. Eyebrow Lamination is a procedure used to re-direct your eyebrow hair's growth, making all of the hairs in the eyebrows be pointed upwards. Eyebrow Lamination is a semi-permanent, non-invasive (does not require any needles) solution that you can get done at your esthetician's office.

But if you are after a temporary and low-commitment solution, a strong brow gel can give you a similar effect. Just use a spoolie to brush out all of your eyebrow hair entirely upwards – the gel will keep them in place for the whole day. This will give your eyebrows a fuller, flawless look.

Microblading
Microblading is a semi-permanent eyebrow-enhancing technique that aims to draw the perfect, permanent eyebrows on your face. You can think of microblading as a tattoo that is not as deep as a regular tattoo.

This procedure is (and should be!) carried out by a salon technician. He/She will measure your face, draw the perfect eyebrows, and then use micro-needles to deposit the pigments in the skin's upper layer. The eyebrows should not be colored in; they should be drawn using hair-like strokes to make the eyebrows look natural and realistic.

If you're thinking about getting your eyebrows microbladed, I have one piece of advice for you: do not go cheap! Ensure you are going to a licensed professional, and look through their portfolio and make sure that you like their work.

Ombre Shading
Ombré shading is a semi-permanent eyebrow styling technique similar to microblading, but with a bit of a different end result. Ombré shading creates a soft-shaded brow pencil look using a small machine to imbed tiny dots of pigment into the skin.

Ombré shading is friendly for all skin types, and it requires fewer touch-up appointments.

Getting your eyebrows ombré shaded will save you time in the morning, and it will keep you from that frustrating feeling of your eyebrows being stubbornly uneven.

The Art of Makeup

Tips Every Woman Needs to Know
It can be a bit intimidating and somewhat confusing for anyone just starting out in the world of make-up. Can you believe that our grandmas used to apply her lipstick as blush, lipstick, and eyeshadow? And nowadays, there are so many eyeshadow palettes, blush palettes, contour palettes, and lipsticks out there that you can feel overloaded with information. That can certainly make a beginner want to give up. Nevertheless, here is the thing- make-up should always be fun!

Make-up should not be complicated or require you to spend your monthly salary on it! Always keep that in mind when you go to purchase some!

Most women have unique relationships with make-up that tend to change and evolve during their lives. If you are applying make-up every day for years and years, you are bound to learn some tricks of the trade and make your own shortcuts to make the job easier for yourself.

If you are in a rush, you should take my advice - I have taken all of the routes possible and tried more make-up products than you can imagine, and I am here to share what I have learned.

Do not overspend or buy items you don't need.
Without a doubt, this is one of the best pieces of advice that you can receive when it comes to make-up: do NOT buy many expensive, high-end products you do not need. However, you do want to buy quality products. Skin is the largest organ, so be conscious of what products you use on it. Getting the hang of the make-up world is and should be all about testing the waters and seeing what works for you, your skin's needs, and your preferences.

Buy samples of the products you are trying out.
If you are looking into finding your new favorite beauty product, you should always buy it in a sample size first. Even though sample sizes are more expensive than buying a full size, they are definitely cheaper than wasting money on the product you do not need! Once you are sure that you like the product, you can then buy it in full size.

Make skincare a priority.
Make-up will look beautiful and seamless only if the skin underneath it is hydrated and healthy, which is why skincare needs to be a priority for every make-up lover. Learning your skin type (oily, combination, dry) and how to take care of it is the first step you should take once you start getting into makeup.

My first tip applies here as well; you should not buy skincare products just because they are popular or because a lot of your friends or favorite celebrities use them. Those products may or may not work for your skin and its needs. You should always remember that your skin is forever changing. It is essential to continually evaluate what is working for it and what needs to be removed from your skincare routine.

Make-up tools are your friend.
Using the applicators that come in make-up kits or your fingers is not the best idea. Even though they will definitely do the job when you are in a rush or have no other (read better) choice, how your makeup looks have a lot to do with how it is applied and the tools you are using to apply it. Wherever you are in your make-up journey, you should invest in a good set of make-up brushes and sponges. Of course, the set's size will depend on your make-up ambitions and needs, but a simple set that contains a few brushes for the eyeshadows and a few face brushes will do the job perfectly well. Applying your make-up with high-quality tools will help it be more natural and well-blended.

Wash your make-up tools often.
While we are on the subject of make-up brushes and sponges, I think it is essential to mention that they absolutely NEED to wash them regularly and properly. Dirty and unhygienic make-up brushes and sponges can lead to acne and even fungal infections. All that caring for your skin and all the expensive skincare products and procedures can be wasted just by a quick swipe of a dirty brush. It is essential to keep your make-up brushes clean and bacteria-free if you want your skin to look healthy and flawless.

Do not underestimate concealer.

If you do not like wearing a foundation daily, a good concealer is all you will need. It will hide all the imperfections and spots, and given that most of us do not always get the recommended amount of sleep, it will be your best friend when it comes to hiding our dark and puffy under-eye area. Finding a concealer that works well for your skin is vital in making your skin look great. When it comes to picking a concealer color, go for two shades lighter than your skin color.

If you are wearing lipstick, always use a lip liner.

Lip liners are designed to help your lipstick last longer and prevent its feathering and bleeding. You should start by lining the outside of your lips with lip liner and fill in the rest of your lips with the lipstick you will be using. Make sure that your lip liner and lipstick are in the same (or very similar) shade. If you want to create an ombre look, you can select a deeper shade lipliner.

Beauty Reflections:

What did you discover about yourself?
What action will you take?

He has made everything Beautiful in its time. Ecclesiastes 3:11

_____

_____

_____

_____

_____

_____

_____

_____

_____

Chapter 5

Lifestyle

Hosting For a Small Gathering

Don't be afraid to invite your friends and family to your home for a party or holiday gathering. Celebrate with these budget-friendly ideas:

Party food

- Soup's on: A good hearty bowl of soup is a great way to feed a crowd. Many soups call for inexpensive ingredients like veggies, potatoes, meat and pasta. As a bonus, most soups can be made a day in advance and reheated before the party, giving you more time to focus on appetizers, beverages and last-minute details. Alternatively, you can also prepare soup in a slow cooker, which has always been a favorite because it cooks all day without additional supervision and stays warm for as long as you need it. Hearty party soups include chili, potato soup, white bean soup, minestrone, savory cheese soup, and broccoli and cheddar soup. Serve with a loaf of French bread, crusty rolls, or garlic bread for a complete meal.

- Sandwiches for the win: Everybody loves a good sandwich, but with different types of bread, fillings, and condiments, serving sandwiches for a party can be time-intensive, messy, and expensive. So, keep it simple. Buy some croissants or ciabatta bread and set out with bowls of chicken salad, tuna salad or egg salad that you prepared in advance. Add a platter of crisp lettuce and fresh tomatoes along with salt and pepper or other savory seasonings and a few different types of chips, and dinner is done.

- Instead of a holiday dinner, consider hosting a brunch or breakfast instead. Breakfast foods like quiche, biscuits, pancakes, waffles, creamy grits are easy to prepare, and everyone loves them! To complete the presentation, add some fresh in-season fresh fruit, some muffins, homemade banana or zucchini bread, or coffee cake.

- A make-your-own bar. This is an excellent concept for a casual get-together because you can decide how simple or fancy you want to get and how many different toppings to serve to fit your budget. Guests love it because they get to prepare the food based on their preference. Food that works well for this concept include:

- Potatoes (served with sour cream, bacon bits, pulled chicken or pork, your preference, cheddar cheese, butter, taco meat, salsa, chili, ham, diced herbs, green onions, broccoli, and black beans), etc.

- Tacos (served with shredded chicken or beef, seasoned hamburger, lettuce, tomatoes, sour cream, onions, shredded cheese, jalapenos, soft flour tortillas, hard taco shells, tortilla chips, black beans, avocado, refried beans, cooked fajita veggies, roasted peppers)

- Pizza. Have guests prepare them, and then you bake or grill them. Serve with prepared pizza crust, tomato sauce, alfredo sauce, pepperoni, cooked crumbled sausage, diced ham, cooked bacon, cooked shredded chicken, cheddar cheese, mozzarella cheese, green and red bell peppers, jalapenos, onions, tomatoes, oregano, basil, mushrooms, pineapple)

- Omelets. Guests select their toppings in a bowl; then, you prepare individually. Serve with diced ham, cooked bacon, crumbled breakfast sausage, shaved steak, cheddar cheese, mozzarella cheese, Monterey Jack cheese, Swiss cheese, sour cream, tomatoes, mushrooms, broccoli, fresh herbs, shallots, onions.

- Rice bowls (served with white rice, brown rice, cilantro-lime rice, diced green onions, diced tomatoes, chopped red and green bell peppers, shaved steak, roasted peppers, mushrooms, asparagus, salsa, chili, soy sauce, Braggs aminos, shrimp and teriyaki)

- Pasta. Keep it simple (spaghetti with tomato sauce, baked ziti or linguine with a quick Pomodoro sauce) or make it more upscale (seafood pasta with shrimp, crab). Serve with salad and a baguette or garlic bread.

- Stick to one meat. Whether it's a turkey, ham or roast, commit to one type of meat and then serve with lots of inexpensive side dishes like potatoes, cooked vegetables, veggie platter, fresh fruit salad, stuffing, casserole, bread, salad. To mix it up a bit, invest in upscale meat, like Cornish hens, lamb chops, or salmon and skip the appetizers.

- Create a signature beverage in a punch bowl. Individual sodas, fancy waters, and ice teas can easily break a budget. Instead, prepare lemonade, homemade or store-bought eggnog, punch, or another pleasing concoction in a large punch bowl.

- Don't forget about dessert. Cookies, brownies, and ice cream are definitely budget-friendly, but if you're looking for something more elegant, consider banana pudding, fresh berries with cream, chocolate truffles, a simple

bundt cake, or a fruit tart.
- Spend time on side dishes. Often an afterthought, side dishes can make or break a meal. Instead of frozen veggies or prepared potato salad, grill some asparagus, roast brussels sprouts, collard greens, or prepare homemade mashed potatoes, candied yams, or macaroni & cheese. Carefully coordinate your side dishes with the main entrée.
- Go with homemade. Catering and preparing dishes are easy solutions but they add up fast. Make your party extra special by making a few dishes from scratch – your guests will appreciate the effort! Think homemade bread (even if you use a bread machine), fresh salsa, homemade salad dressing, or cobbler from scratch.

Decorations

Decorating for a party can seem daunting when you're trying to watch your spending. Here are some great ideas to help you pull a fantastic atmosphere together.

- Clean. You may think it's common sense to mention, but a thorough cleaning and rearranging of items can greatly impact a room. Hide power and charging cords, clean out the closet for guest's coats.
- Create a beautiful grouping of candles to add a soft glow. Candles are relatively inexpensive, or just use what you have on hand.
- Buy fabric remnants and use them as festive table runners or tablecloths, buy chair covers for your dining room

chairs and select a beautiful centerpiece for your table.

- For a holiday party, cheap wrapping paper is your friend. Wrap different sizes of empty Amazon boxes, add festive bows and use them as a centerpiece or place them in corners of the room. Use big bows to decorate kitchen cabinets.
- Take a trip to the dollar store. You'll be amazed by all the great finds, including faux flowers, vases, marbles, decorative signs, ribbons, banners, accent pieces, picture frames and more.
- Mix and match your serving ware. Find unique pieces at stores like Ross Dress for Less, garage sales, and thrift stores.
- Make a photo collage with memories of you and your guests to hang on the wall.
- Craft place cards from pinecones and ribbons.
- Ditch the theme. Themes force you to search high and low for specific accessories, and that can cost a lot!
- Make the food the focus. Buy or borrow different serving platters and bowls so you can create a serving space that is pleasing to the eye. Make it more interesting by adding height with a cake platter, small wooden crates, or tiered serving plates.
- Balloons are fun and cheap. Group in corners and skip youthful primary colors in favor of pastels or rich golds, browns, and reds.

Crafts/Activities

- Have guests help you decorate your Christmas tree, I have had a few tree trimming parties, that were a ton of fun.
- Ask guests to bring a few toiletries and pack boxes for a local charity.
- Fill a mason jar with M&M candies or coins. Ask guests to guess how many candies or how much money are in the jar. The one with the closest number wins the jar filled with candy or money.
- Photobooth: Hang wrapping paper on a wall to serve as your background. Provide seasonal decorations, scarves, sunglasses, or more to use as photo props.
- Have a cookie swap. Ask each guest to bring a few dozen homemade cookies, provide the packaging, and swap cookies.
- Play board games.
- Go for a walk around the neighborhood.
- Set the table with a plain white fabric tablecloth and provide guests with fabric markers. Make sure you have a protective barrier between the fabric and the table. Ask them to pen holiday memories or best wishes. Add the year and use it as a conversation starter at future parties.

Games

- Go retro and play charades, catchphrase, uno
- Provide a large tablet of drawing paper and play Pictionary on a larger scale.
- Gather fun, little-known facts about guests on a card, then read aloud and ask everyone to guess who the cards describe.
- If it's nice outside, play old-fashioned kids games – you'll have fun! Think obstacle courses, bean bag tosses, and sack races.
- Print out bingo cards and award prizes.
- Engage in a lively game of lie, lie, and truth. Guests share two lies and one truth about themselves, and the others have to figure out which "fact" is true.
- Create conversation cards to use as icebreakers. Come up with open-ended questions, write on small cards, and place them in a jar or basket. Have guests make a random selection and respond.
- Story starters. You start a fictional story, and then as you go around the room, each guest embellishes upon the plot.

Game prize and party favor ideas

If you want to hand out prizes to the winners or party favors to guests, consider these ideas:
- Large candy bars
- Colorful pens

- Sparkling Cider
- Truffles
- Candles
- Small succulent plants
- Decorative soaps
- Fun stress balls
- Key chain flashlights
- Mini hand lotions
- Small bottles of hand sanitizer
- Popcorn
- Bags of fancy nuts

Other party tips and ideas

Make your party truly special and save cold, hard cash at the same time with these tips:

- Use your graphic design skills to create a digital invitation and then text or email. You'll save money on invitations and postage.
- Load your smartphone with a playlist of music for the evening.
- Know your guests. Ask about any food allergies. If you have pets, let them know. Also, consider access to your home for guests with disabilities.
- Keep the temperature indoors cool as crowds will quickly generate extra heat. If it's hot or cold outdoors, place fans, candles, or heaters around. You can even start a bonfire in a fire pit. Make guests as comfortable as possible.
- Splurge on one item that is important to you and then keep the rest on budget. You may want to focus on a fancy non-alcoholic beverage, a special bakery cake.
- Create a budget and plan accordingly. It's impossible to

stay on budget if you don't have one! Even small items will add up quickly.

- Don't skip self-care. Planning a party can take a lot of time and effort. Don't forget to plan your attire and leave plenty of time for a shower and hair and makeup preparation ahead of guests arriving (even those who are early)!
- Accept offers of help. Sure, you want to take care of everyone and make sure they have a good time, but let them if someone offers to help clean up or refill the beverages. Helping gives guests something to do and makes them feel good.
- Create a party box. As you clean up and put items away, salvage what you can for a future party. Eventually, you'll acquire a treasure trove of tablecloths, serving dishes, carafes, and other items that will come in handy next time you entertain. Ask me how I know!

Hosting Check List

One month before the party:
____ Set a day and time
____ Make a budget
____ Create a guest list
____ Create and send invitations
____ Decide on games and activities
____ Establish a menu
____ Make a food shopping list and start buying non-perishables
____ Purchase game prizes and party favors

___ Ask friends and family to borrow items like tents, tables/chairs, and linens

___ Choose party games

___ Create a budget

___ Decide on a signature non-alcoholic drink

___ Recruit friends and family to help, if needed

___ Download music on a smartphone or iPhone

___ Take a trip to the dollar store for decor

Two weeks before the party:

___ Finish shopping for non-perishable grocery items

___ Purchase paper party supplies

___ Purchase game prizes

___ Purchase decorations

___ Print bingo cards

___ Ask guests about allergies and other potential areas of concerns

___ Clean the house

___ Wrap empty boxes to resemble packages

___ Create Charades slips

___ Ask guests for unique facts to share for the game

___ Print bingo cards online

___ Create conversation cards for a game

One week before the party:

___ Fill and count M&Ms or Money for the jar

___ Bake cake

___ Wash glassware

___ Press linens, if using your own

___ Access serving dishes, and utensils, if using your own

___ Create photo booth area, layout props

___ Prepare party favor bags

___ Make place cards
___ Assemble Christmas decorations for decorating
___ Gather game/activity supplies

Day before the party:
___ Shop for fresh, perishable grocery items
___ Blow-up balloons
___ Cut up fruit/veggies
___ Make and chill drinks
___ Organize party space, re-arrange furniture
___ Prep dessert
___ Prep any appetizers, breads, or dishes that can be made ahead of time

Morning of party:
___ Shower and get dressed
___ Put out yard signs
___ Hang streamers
___ Hang garland
___ Organize food table
___ Prepare party food
___ Set up games
___ Gather together game items
___ Set up an obstacle course
___ Decorate party area
___ Charge phone or camera

Shopping List

Details are critical when you're planning a special event. To make sure you have everything needed, here's a convenient shopping list:

Food

If you're preparing a soup:

___ Large soup pot
___ Soup ingredients
___ Ladle
___ Soup bowls and spoons

For sandwiches:

___ Your choice of bread
___ Your favorite sandwich fillings or ingredients to make them
___ Condiments like mayonnaise and mustard
___ Accoutrements like lettuce, tomatoes, and pickles

Ingredients for a fruit/veggie platter:

___ Fruit or veggie dip
___ Black olives
___ Baby carrots
___ Cherry tomatoes
___ Red, yellow or orange bell peppers
___ Pineapple chunks
___ Strawberries
___ Blueberries
___ Cantaloupe
___ Cucumbers
___ Zucchini

___ Green bell peppers
___ Kiwi
___ Green grapes
___ Broccoli
___Green apples
___ Pears
___ Apples

For Potato bar:
___ Sour cream
___ Bacon bits
___ Pulled pork
___ Pulled Chicken
___ Your choice of cheese
___ Butter
___ Taco meat
___ Ham
___ Diced herbs
___ Green onions
___ Black beans
___ Broccoli
___ Chili
___ Salsa

For Taco bar:
___ Spiced shredded chicken or beef
___ Seasoned hamburger
___ Lettuce
___ Tomatoes
___ Sour cream
___ Onions
___ Shredded cheese
___ Jalapenos

____ Lime slices
____ Soft flour tortillas
____ Hard taco shells
____ Tortilla chips
____ Black beans
____ Avocado
____ Refried beans
____ Cooked fajita veggies
____ Roasted Bell peppers

For Pizza bar:
____ Prepared pizza crust
____ Tomato sauce
____ Alfredo sauce
____ Pepperoni
____ Cooked crumbled sausage
____ Diced ham
____ Cooked bacon
____ Cooked shredded chicken
____ Pulled pork
____ Cheddar cheese
____ Mozzarella cheese
____ Green and red bell peppers
____ Jalapenos
____ Onions
____Tomatoes
____ Oregano
____ Basil
____ Mushrooms
____ Pineapple

For Omelet bar:

___ Diced ham
___ Cooked bacon
___ Crumbled breakfast sausage
___ Shaved steak
___ Cheddar cheese
___ Mozzarella cheese
___ Monterey Jack cheese
___ Swiss cheese
___ Sour cream
___ Tomatoes
___ Mushrooms
___ Broccoli
___ Fresh herbs
___ Shallots
___ Onions

For Rice bowls:

___ White rice
___ Brown rice
___ Cilantro lime rice
___ Diced green onion
___ Diced tomatoes
___ Chopped red and green bell peppers
___ Shaved steak
___ Bell peppers
___ Mushrooms
___ Salsa
___ Chili
___ Soy sauce
___ Braggs Aminos
___ Shrimp

___ Teriyaki
___ Appetizes
___ Side dishes
___ Beverages
___ Dessert
___ Bread
___ Cleaning supplies
___ Eggs, enough for egg race
___ Giant candy bars, for game prizes

Paper Supplies (if using)

___ Paper plates
___ Paper cups
___ Plastic forks
___ Plastic spoons
___ Plastic knives
___ Toothpicks
___ Napkins
___ Cake paper plates
___ Small cake or beverage napkins
___ Napkin holder
___ Utensil holder
___ Tablecloths or table coverings
___ Card box

Party Supplies

___ Save the Date cards
___ Invitations
___ Game prizes
___ Thank you notes
___ Candles
___ Cake decorations
___ Cupcake liners

___ Cake platter, server
___ Ice cream scoop
___ Coffee maker
___ Punch bowl

<u>Decorations</u>
___ Candles
___ Fabric remnants
___ Wrapping paper
___ Ribbon
___ Serving pieces
___ Orange slices
___ Pinecones
___ Balloons
___ Balloon weights
___ Centerpieces
___ Confetti
___ Streamers
___ Garland
___ Yard signs

<u>Games/Activities</u>
For photo booth background and accessories
___ Wrapping paper
___ Scarves
___ Sunglasses

<u>For guessing game supplies:</u>
___ M&Ms
___ Mason jar
___ Paper for guessing strips
___ Board games
___ Jigsaw puzzle

For cookie decorating
___ Frosting
___ Sprinkles
___ Edible markers
___ Plain sugar cookies

For creative tablecloth
___ Plain white fabric tablecloth
___ Fabric markers

Games
For Pictionary:
___ Large drawing tablets
___ Pencils and pens

For backyard games:
___ Burlap bags for a sack race
___ Bean bags for bean bag toss

For bingo:
___ Bingo card sheets
___ Bingo markers
___ Large candy bars for prizes

Prizes
___ Large candy bars
___ Colorful pens
___ Truffles
___ Candles
___ Small succulent plants
___ Decorative soaps
___ Fun stress balls
___ Key chain flashlights

___ Mini hand lotions
___ Small bottles of hand sanitizer
___ Shot glasses
___ Bags of fancy nuts

Beauty Reflections:

What did you discover about yourself?
What action will you take?

He has made everything Beautiful in its time. Ecclesiastes 3:11

_____

_____

_____

_____

_____

_____

_____

_____

_____

_____

Chapter 6

Marriage Preparation
Proper Dating

How It Started...

When God made you, He put something extraordinary in you. I'm not talking about talents or gifts; those are a wonderful blessing from the Lord, but those aren't our main focus. Right now, I'm talking of the desire God put in you as a woman. It was put there before the fall, but God spoke of it once more after.

This is recorded in Genesis 3:16 GNB.;
*"And He said to the woman, 'I will increase your trouble in pregnancy and your pain in giving birth. **In spite of this, you will still have desire for your husband**, yet you will be subject to him.'"*

This was God speaking. In the "curse," as we call it, hope for man. So, although there was a pain to come, God gave hope. The woman will have the desire for her husband.

God made the man desire the woman, and the woman to desire the man in return. So, the feeling is mutual and should result in a marriage. However, there's a process before marriage, and today we know it by two names; dating or courting.

This is how the English dictionary defines;

Dating: date regularly; have a steady relationship with.

Courting: a man's courting of a woman; seeking the affections of a woman (usually with the hope of marriage).

How is your relationship currently defined?

These are according to the Advanced English Dictionary. However, some dictionaries include the possibility of romance, and rightly so, because that's the process for those in the world. For them, it's a place to exchange feelings, passions, and desires in ungodly manners.

Proper Christian Dating

So, the believer's definition must be consistent with God's definition, and in God's definition, there are no sexual activities added to the definition.

The Christian sister who is in a relationship that intends to grow into a marriage must do things differently from how the world would do it.

Dating, which possibly leads to marriage, is an interesting period and important in any person's life. When that time comes for a relationship that should metamorphose into a marriage by the will of God, how do you go about it as a lady?

The media has sadly taken hold of things and spun them out of the original course God intended. The idea of dating is not left out!

Many ideas are flying about based on people's opinions rather than the opinion of God. People say it's okay to have kisses, it's okay to have sex, and it's okay to do a bunch of stuff. But, what does God say?

This is the task of the modern believer – finding and abiding in the will of God.

What Does the Bible Say About Dating?

The New Testament may not have dealt thoroughly with the topic of dating, but if you look carefully, I think there are no secrets to what is expected of us.

The commands and instructions for living in the Old Testament gave clear instructions that speak about the dating/ courtship period or period of promise (when a virgin was promised or betrothed to a man to be married – what we'd call courtship today). It says that they must do so in the absence of sexual immorality, and every form of sexual immorality was punishable. *Exodus 20:14.*

God has always been vocal about the need for purity from sexual sins, and that hasn't changed even with the colossal changes the world has undergone. You must ask yourself how God wants things.

You need to ask, "In my courtship with this brother, what can I and can't I do? What are my boundaries?"

These are wise questions that will greatly help you.

The bible says in the book of 1 Corinthians 7:2 ESV;

"But because of the temptation to sexual immorality, each man should have his own wife and each woman her own husband."

So, you're dating, and you're preparing to get married, and that's good. It's biblical!

However, one of the reasons for marriage is to avoid sexual immorality. Therefore, you must do all you can with the help of God to avoid it while you're dating. This is a dangerous period as the devil tries every possible trick to make you fail in your decision to please God with your body.

Characteristics of a Godly Man

Setting standards has never been ungodly, so you should!

If you can set standards in every aspect of your life, from the kind of school you attended to the color of your phone's pouch, then I think having standards for a husband is also in place.

It only becomes a problem when your standards are either too unrealistic or aren't in line with the opinion of God.

So, what are the qualities you should be looking out for? Good question!

If you're already dating, it's not too late to use this guide. Of course, in addition, you must weigh the extent of your compatibility with this partner. However, I believe there are standards that a Christian woman should look out for in a man she intends to accept as a husband, and these are scriptural qualities that should be considered:

Love
Remember that as much as he's "your" husband, you also have a family he'll relate with, even as limited as it might be. Secondly, you must remember that you'll have kids, and he'll be their father. How much of God is formed in him? I say "How much of God" because God is love, and if any man must know how to love, he must know God first. *1 John 4:7-8,20-21.*

Joy
Is this man of a joyous spirit, or is he easily crushed and devastated? I'm talking about the genuine joy that comes from the Spirit, the one that's not controlled by the things that he has or what he sees. I'm talking about a man who knows God and is hopeful of what He can do tomorrow regardless of what today looks like.

Peace
You must check if the cares of life easily steal his peace. If he's down today, how does he treat you? How does he treat those around him? Is there inner peace that is governed by a godly understanding? Pay attention to these.

Patience
When things are not going his way, how patient is he? Not only with circumstances around him, but how patient is he with you when you make mistakes? Be careful to avoid impatient men.

Kindness
What is his opinion on kindness? Does he think it's just some extinct virtue that's no longer needed in this generation? Does he look to help people around him? Does he care about those who are not as privileged as him?

Goodness
Is he good to those around him? Is he good to your family and you? Is he graceful and constrained by compassion in his dealings with others?

Faithfulness
What is his attitude towards consistency and diligence? Can he be trusted? Is he faithfully walking and working with God? Any man that gets genuine faithfulness with God right will also find no problem being faithful to you.

Gentleness
Gentleness is not just being slow to act. It's a combination of kindness, patience, and self-control. Do you see him having these characters evident? A gentleman will also be willing to help you even with the house chores. He'll be willing to support you in anything you need.

Self-control
Control of self. Contrary to what people think, you can have control over yourself with the help of the Holy Spirit. Can he control his temper, acting patiently when he should lash out, for example? Can he control his sexual urges and keep them under check? Is he disciplined enough to control his actions?

In my opinion, these are the ultimate qualities you should search for in any man. Why? Because if you have noticed,

these are characters that the bible calls, "the fruit of the Spirit" in *Galatians 5:22-23 ESV;*
"But the fruit of the Spirit is love, joy, peace, patience, kindness, goodness, faithfulness, gentleness, self-control; against such things there is no law."

It's that simple, if you're a Christian sister seeking a godly man, how else to know but by the expression of the Spirit of God in him?

The bible says that if you find anyone with these characters, you are safe because there's no law against these, meaning there's no cause for concern because such a person expresses who God is. Wouldn't that make a wonderful husband? You agree, right!

Although, in reality, we might still be struggling with the flesh allowing the Spirit to express one or more of these characters. In essence, when you see a man that's serious with God and walking with God to being transformed, even if you don't see all of these characters expressed at the highest level, you'll know he's serious about being better.

In all, these are the absolutes you should be looking out for in a husband because any man that gets it right with God is a safe zone.

Setting Proper Boundaries

Now you're dating, but you fear God and wouldn't want to hurt him by the sin of sexual immorality or anything else. This is where boundaries will help you.

Boundaries are what help us attain any potential achievements no matter what we are trying to accomplish. In dating, you also need them. You need to know what to do and what not. The mistake you'll make is thinking everything will work itself out. As long as you've decided to have a godly relationship that should glorify God, the devil will come for you.

The biggest temptation in a relationship between two unmarried people is that of sexual immorality. What is sexual immorality?

It's any way in which a sexual act is conducted in the wrong way. So, for an unmarried couple, that means engaging in any romantic activities that should be mentioned only between married people. Examples of these can include wet kissing (if this is a strong trigger, eliminate it), romance, sexting, having sex, and every other invention that the world has come up with that shares intimacy between two people.

Although sexual immorality does not only apply to unmarried people, this is what we mean in this context.
So, how do you overcome or avoid these instances? You need to set boundaries.

These are a few things you can do:

Strive For Pure Thoughts
Guard your mind, and constrain it to only think what is good and pure. *Philippians 4:8.*
Every sin and equally every act that glorifies God indeed starts from the heart. The heart is the powerhouse of any person. It's out of the heart that either good or evil comes from. Jesus said in *Matthew 15:19 ESV;*

*"**For out of the heart come** evil thoughts, murder, **adultery, sexual immorality,** theft, false witness, slander."*

This means if you can keep your heart pure and clear of these thoughts that eventually manifest in the flesh, then you can avoid them. The sin of sexual immorality starts from the heart. Keep your heart pure and full of God's holiness, and you'll be fine.

Set godly Meeting Hours
You must know what time of the day will be less likely for the devil to overcome you in temptation. Any time of the day is always a time for the devil to try to make us fall, but you'd agree with me that there are times that have a higher possibility. For example, meeting your date at late hours will get thoughts of sexual intimacy higher up than meeting at noon. If you meet at noon over lunch, after that, you will mostly think about getting back to other activities of the day, right? But, say, you meet over dinner, and it gets pretty late, there's a higher tendency to get tempted to spend the night at their or your home. If you're meeting him and his family over dinner, that's safe. You get the idea. Don't put yourself out there for the devil. Emotions are hard to control on a good

day. Why let the devil have an advantage?

Setting The Right Meeting Places

You also need to pay attention to where you meet. As a lady, you should avoid meeting your unmarried partner in the absence of people or in a private setting. Always make sure you try to meet him where there are other godly friends present. Make sure you try to avoid being alone in a room together. Don't be ignorant of the schemes of the devil. It is not wise to let someone you've just met pick you up from your home. We often hear about stalkers, and those who don't have your best interest at heart become aggressive when you've decided that it's best if the two of you move on and they don't agree and have your address! It puts you in a very vulnerable state. Give the relationship time to see if this is your life mate. I would say a least six months. It is not as easy if things don't go well for you to pick up suddenly and move. Dating is for collecting data; when you have collected enough data one way or the other, you act on it.

Restrict Intimate Discussions To The Barest Minimum

I know it's fun discussing things that express strong emotions, like saying how much you love your partner and how much you'd sacrifice for them. I want you to know that you're in a serious battle with the devil for your purity. The devil will use every strategy to make your relationship unpleasing to God by introducing sexual sins at every opportunity he gets. So, you need to be wise as well. Make sure you avoid discussions that will get your imagination stirred. Naturally, when you are in the company of the one you love, your hormones are already raging, so you need to be extra careful not to trigger anything that completes the circuit. Whether it's on a call, texting, or in person, keep discussions clear of romance and things that can spark emotional tension. It's challenging to do so, but God's help is available. Listen, Sis. My head is not stuck off in the sand. My husband and I had to be very intentional about this 22 years ago. There were days I got put out, and days he got put out. It was TIME TO GO right NOW, lol.

Build Godly Company
This is as valid as every other point here because as much as you try to do all of these things, one wrong opinion from a close friend can destroy everything. Don't surround yourself with people who don't think like you. If you're trying to nurture godly thoughts, hang around godly people as well because "Bad company ruins good morals." [*1 Corinthians 15:33*].

Dating or courting is a good system a man and a woman who intend to get married will pass through. It's a time to know who you are planning to spend your life with. Some temptations come within this period, trials as well as discouragements, but trust in God. Always seek God's opinion and let Him lead you as He blesses your union and makes it established.

Beauty Reflections:

What did you discover about yourself?
What action will you take?

He has made everything Beautiful in its time. Ecclesiastes 3:11

_____

_____

_____

_____

_____

_____

_____

_____

_____

_____

_____

As I conclude this Beauty Guide, my heart is so full. As I get older, I tell you, Sis, my sensitivity is heightened, and my heart is greatly impacted. My prayer for you is that you navigated to some areas in your life and your heart that you never thought to be beautiful. Coming away with new discoveries about yourself that will lead you to make choices that create a greater sense of the wholeness and internal beauty God intended for you.

May God Richly Bless You,
LaDonna Roberts

Join My Free Community Facebook Group

ALL THINGS BEAUTIFUL - INSIDE & OUT

If you want to continue to learn how to make
All Things Beautiful Inside & Out, then this community is for you.

In This Private Group:
I will interact with those that have read my book
I will go live in this group
Host Q & A sessions
Give away free resources

For New Product Releases, And Services:
Patent Pending Lash System
Holiday Meals from Scratch made Easy Cookbook
Master Eyelash Course for Professionals
Speaking Engagements & Coaching Sessions

Go to my Website at www.LaDonnaRoberts.com to get added to my email list.

Also, connect with me on 📷 @LadyLaDonnaRoberts

About the Author

LaDonna Roberts – Bio

For over 18 years, LaDonna Roberts has been a Beauty Professional and Lash Enhancement Expert. She's grown to become one of the most respected Make-up Artist and Esthetician in the Industry, servicing global icons such as Serena Williams, Meagan Good, Lauren London, Lady Gaga, LaLa Anthony and many more.

As her passion grew, LaDonna swiftly transitioned and redirected her focus to the Beauty Industry after establishing her origins as a Film Exec. She found the Beauty Industry to be significantly more rewarding due to her ability to enhance and empower her clientele. As she enhanced their external beauty she also advocated for the discovery of internal beauty and wholeness that she believes is available to everyone. LaDonna always says "Everything you touch with intention can be made beautiful" ©

In 2010, LaDonna's health took an abrupt turn for the worst when cancer attacked her body. Unfortunately, preventing her from doing what fulfilled her most. This news was surprisingly & seemingly devastating but she never lost faith. Eight days after the diagnosis, she went in for a second screening & was met with miraculous news, the doctor reported that there was no longer any evidence of cancer in her body. She credits receiving the Abrahamic covenant promise, coupled with nourishing her physical body with alkaline water, whole food nutrition, and holistic modalities for her being healed twice, emotionally, and physically. Thanks to this transformation, LaDonna has been an advocate of receiving God's promises and whole food nutrition ever since.

Today, LaDonna is now bringing her knowledge and experiences to life on the pages of her various books. Her first book, All Things Beautiful, Inside and Out – Your Beauty Guide to Wholeness will publish March 2022. She has also collaborated with eleven other dynamic women of faith to tell their stories of how they overcame. In this LaDonna hopes the content of these books will encourage and inspire others to have unwavering faith when chasing their dreams & God given destiny.

www.ingramcontent.com/pod-product-compliance
Lightning Source LLC
Chambersburg PA
CBHW072158270326
41930CB00011B/2473